D0184678

JUST Like MUM Says

A Book of Mum's Wit

Rosemarie Jarski

EBURY
PRESS

JUST Like MUM Says

A Book of Mum's Wit

Rosemarie Jarski

EBURY
PRESS

1 3 5 7 9 10 8 6 4 2

Published in 2009 by Ebury Press, an imprint of Ebury Publishing
A Random House Group company

The Random House Group Limited Reg. No. 954009

Addresses for companies within the Random House Group can be
found at www.randomhouse.co.uk

A CIP catalogue record for this book is available from
the British Library

The Random House Group Limited supports The Forest Stewardship
Council (FSC), the leading international forest certification
organisation. All our titles that are printed on Greenpeace approved
FSC certified paper carry the FSC logo. Our paper procurement policy
can be found at www.rbooks.co.uk/environment

Mixed Sources
Product group from well-managed
forests and other controlled sources
www.fsc.org   Cert no. TT-COC-2139
© 1996 Forest Stewardship Council

Printed in the UK by CPI Mackays, Chatham, ME5 8TD

ISBN 9780091930486

To buy books by your favourite authors and register for offers visit
www.rbooks.co.uk

To the Best Mum in the World

This is our mother. Pray for us.

Tagline, Mermaids

Contents

What is a mother?

Piles are a Jewish man's affliction. Piles and mothers. What causes them?

Stephen Fry, The Hippopotamus

We really have no definition of 'mother' in our law books. 'Mother' was believed to have been so basic that no definition was deemed necessary.

Marianne O. Battani, US Judge

Mother is food; she is love; she is warmth; she is earth.

Erich Fromm

A mother is a nutritionist, a child psychologist, an engineer, a production manager, an expert buyer, all in one.

Margaret Mead

Women who miscalculate are called 'mother'.

Abigail Van Buren

The maternal stereotypes: the martyr, the boardroom zombie and the Chelsea tractor Boudicca, fighting to the death to get her children into the right clarinet class.

Mary Riddell

I never had a mother. I suppose a mother is one to whom you hurry when you are troubled.

Emily Dickinson

My son, Kyle, 4, was unsuccessfully trying to open a bottle of children's vitamins. After watching several vain attempts, I explained: 'It's made so only mommies and daddies can open it.' After tiring of his struggle, Kyle relinquished the bottle. As I easily opened it for him, Kyle stared in amazement and asked in a breathless voice, 'How does it know you're a mommy?'

Angela Mitchell

You're not a mother until you've had nits.

Coleen Nolan, Loose Women

You know you're a mother when… you make a cup of coffee and drink it cold; you sign a cheque with a crayon; you wipe other kids' noses.

Anon

You know you really are a mother when: you use your own saliva to clean your child's face; your child throws up and you catch it.

Erma Bombeck

A mother is someone who maintains the impression that she truly prefers the heel of the bread, the crust of the pie, the cookies with burned bottoms, and the chair with the wobbly leg.

Patrick Regan

A mother is she who can take the place of all others, but whose place no one else can take.

Cardinal Mermillod

A mother! What are we really? They all grow up
whether we look after them or not.

Christina Stead

The second oldest profession: Motherhood

Motherhood – the second oldest profession and the
biggest on-the-job training programme.

Erma Bombeck

The common fallacy among women is that simply
having children makes one a mother, which is as
absurd as believing that having a piano makes one a
musician.

Sydney J. Harris

Fallopian tubes and ovaries do not a mother
make.

Oprah Winfrey

You can't qualify in the subject, but you're expected to have a vast number of qualifications: chauffeur, diplomat, vet, clown, *Blue Peter* presenter, chef, paramedic, critic, referee, weapons inspector, therapist, computer expert, liar.

Imogen Stubbs

Motherhood is the state of coping with an infinite series of demands, most of which are invisible to everyone except the mother.

Kate Clanchy

You go to work when you're sick, maybe even clinically depressed, because motherhood is perhaps the only unpaid position where failure to show up can result in arrest.

Mary Kay Blakely

Motherhood... It's the willing acceptance that you will never again – for the next twenty years or so at least – enjoy a leisurely meal, pass two consecutive days without doing laundry, or speak uninterrupted on the phone.

Patrick Regan

It's the best all round job. No other career would allow you to be plumber, drill sergeant, nurse, chef, umpire, banker, telephonist and international diplomat – all before 9.30am.

Anonymous mother

Pregnancy doubled her, birth halved her, and motherhood turned her into Everywoman.

Erica Jong

Motherhood is the most emotional experience of one's life. One joins a kind of woman's mafia.

Janet Suzman

Most days I feel like an acrobat high above a crowd out of which my own parents, my in-laws, potential employers, phantoms of 'other women who do it' and a thousand faceless eyes stare up.

Anonymous mother

It's a dead-end job. You've no sooner learned the skills than you are redundant.

Claire Rayner

Motherhood – an incident, an occupation, or a career, according to the mettle of the women.

Mary C. Beasley

Maybe baby: Family planning

Having a child is surely the most beautiful irrational act that two people in love can commit.

Bill Cosby

You wake up one day and say, 'You know what, I don't think I ever need to sleep or have sex again.' Congratulations, you're ready to have children.

Ray Romano

My mother wants grandchildren, so I said, 'Mom, go for it!'

Sue Murphy

I can't decide if I want a baby. My friends are like, 'Oh you learn all this great stuff, like how to survive on two hours' sleep.' If I want to learn that I'll just become a political prisoner.

Cathryn Michon

I met this guy who said he loved children, then I found out he was on parole for it.

Monica Piper

—Dorothy, what's so great about having children anyway?
—I just want them. It's like you and pints of lager.

Gary and Dorothy, Men Behaving Badly

I want to have children and I know time is running out. I want to have them while my parents are still young enough to take care of them.

Rita Rudner

I'll be a real good mother. I've been called one.

Wendy Liebman

I was asking my friend who has children, 'What if I have a baby and I dedicate my life to it and it grows up to hate me, and it blames everything wrong with its life on me.' And she said, 'What do you mean, if?'

Rita Rudner

My wife and I don't have any kids. We don't want any kids. We're happy the way we are. If we have a sudden urge to spank someone, we'll spank each other.

Daniel Liebert

I can't have children because I have white couches.

Carrie Snow

Parenting may not be for you if ... you consider a Happy Meal to be any meal that includes a dry Martini; you think PTA stands for Pizza Take-Out Association; refrigerator art leaves you cold.

Ellen Metter

Oh, kids ruin everything. I mean look at the stitching on this jacket. You can't trust a ten-year-old to do a good hidden button.

Karen Walker, Will and Grace

I'll never have a baby because I'm afraid I'll leave it on top of my car.

Lizz Winstead

If your parents never had children, chances are you won't either.

Dick Cavett

The greatest advantage of not having children must be that you can go on believing that you are a nice person: once you have children, you realise how wars start.

Fay Weldon

The only way my wife and I could afford to have kids is if she breastfed them for 18 years.

Paul Alexander

What is a home without children? Paid for!

Anon

I want that one! Paths to parenthood

My husband and I have decided to give the advantage of our home to one of your foundlings. Of course, we wouldn't want one that cries.

Mrs Marcus Gilworth, Blossoms in the Dust

Angelina Jolie and Brad Pitt, they never stop adopting kids. I think she has a factory in her basement and when the kids get to be 7 they're put in there to make clothes.

Joan Rivers

Adopting black babies is the latest thing for celebrities because it's really slimming and it goes with everything.

Graham Norton

What I may do is pop over to Rumania or Brazil and bring back something small and disadvantaged. Brazilian babies in particular interest me, as we would be able to keep the kitchen door locked and have them limbo through the cat flap.

Victoria Wood, spoof interview for Ooh! Hello *magazine*

If you have adopted children it is kinder to tell them they are adopted. In fact, someone suggested it would be kinder for me to tell my children they're adopted even though they're not.

Phyllis Diller

I asked my mother if I was adopted. She said, 'Not yet, but we placed an ad.'

Dana Snow

There was once a kindly she-elephant who accidentally stood upon a hen. The elephant was greatly distressed, especially when she looked down and saw all the little chickens running about, cheeping. 'Poor little motherless creatures!' she exclaimed. 'I will be a mother to them!' And gathering the chickens tenderly underneath her, she sat down upon them.

Dictionary of British Folk Tales

When I got my foster son, he was the cutest little guy I'd ever seen, but there was always that little voice at the back of my mind going, 'Remember, the saxophone was in the closet after a month.'

Paula Poundstone

When is the right time to ask someone if you can borrow their uterus? Probably not right after you realise you didn't return their lawn mower.

Cyndi Stiles

They're borrowing one tiny little egg and some space.

Donna Regan, surrogate mother

—Our surrogacy fee is $100,000.
—It costs more to have someone born than to have someone killed!
—It takes longer.

Chaffee Bicknell and Angie Ostrowiski, Baby Mama

The Vatican came down with a new ruling: no surrogate mothers. Good thing they didn't make this rule before Jesus was born.

Elayne Boosler

An anonymous woman is offering $15,000 for the sperm of a Stanford student. Boy, when I was in college I couldn't *give* it away.

David Corrado

A woman recently had a baby from an embryo that had been frozen for seven years. She said, 'I had no idea if I was having a little boy, a little girl – or fish fingers.'

Conan O'Brien

Now that we can clone humans they've removed the one pleasurable thing about having a child.

David Letterman

I prefer the old-fashioned way of having children. By accident.

Phyllis Diller

In the pudding club

I got married and we had a baby nine months and ten seconds later.

Jayne Mansfield

She was really surprised to find out that she was pregnant. 'When did you have your last check up?' the doctor asked her. 'Never! An Italian, a Frenchman and a Yank, but never a Czech!'

Anon

Pregnant?! Yeah but no but yeah but no but, no, because I've never had sex apart from that one time eight months ago, but apart from that I'm a complete virgin.

Vicky Pollard, Little Britain

Are you one of those ladies who doesn't realise she's pregnant until she's sitting on the toilet and the kid pops out?

Debbie, Knocked Up

A Man Did This to Me, Oprah

Slogan on the T-shirt of a pregnant woman

—We're going to have a baby. That's my Christmas present to you.
—All I needed was a tie.

Louise and Virgil Starkwell, Take the Money and Run

We told people as soon as we knew ourselves...
Several people guessed anyway because I went
to a Christmas party and was still sober at the end
of it.

Sobernow, mumsnet.com

The shape of things to come

A woman said, 'Do you mind if I sit down because
I'm pregnant.' I said, 'You don't look it. How long
have you been pregnant?' She said, 'Only ten
minutes – but doesn't it make you feel tired?'

Max Miller

I looked up some of the symptoms of pregnancy –
moody, irritable, big bosoms. I've obviously been
pregnant for 36 years.

Victoria Wood

Being pregnant makes you feel like an adolescent girl.
First, you're constantly embarrassed about your

sexuality, because there it is for everybody to see: 'Ha-ha, look at her, she had sex!' Then there's the raging hormones. You're crying one day, laughing the next.

Cathy Crimmins

—During which month do women start showing their pregnancy?
—September?

Host and Contestant, Family Feud, USA

You should never say anything to a woman that even remotely suggests you think she's pregnant unless you can see an actual baby emerging from her at that moment.

Dave Barry

I'd rather see a pregnant woman standing on the bus than a fat girl sitting down crying.

Jimmy Carr

The only time a woman wishes she were a year older is when she is expecting a baby.

Mary Marsh

—Dorothy, are you feeling all right?
—Well, everything's twice as big as it was nine months ago, and I'm growing another head inside me, let's start there.

Tony and Dorothy, Men Behaving Badly

Urgh! There's a midget in my guts doing number twos in my veins, and just after Christmas it's going to try to come out through my la-la! And I haven't been to India yet! Or finished the kitchen!

Caitlin Moran

—Anyone'd think you were the only woman ever to bloody be pregnant. It's only the size of a bloody orange.
—Well, that's as much as you know – it's the size of a grapefruit, thank you, Dave.

Denise and Dave, The Royle Family

In my first pregnancy…I went from a D cup to a FF-cup. When I moaned about this to my dear friend Vic Reeves, his eyes lit up and he asked whether the double F stood for 'Fucking Fantastic'.

Ulrika Jonsson

It's as if somebody is steadily blowing her breasts full of air like a beach ball. I worry that they will explode.

Dan Greenburg

How can I have morning sickness when I don't get up till noon?

Rita Rudner

My mother had morning sickness after I was born.

Rodney Dangerfield

When I was pregnant, my friends sneered, 'Eating for two, are we?' I said, 'Get lost. I'm not cutting down.'

Jo Brand

You know what they say when a supermodel gets pregnant? Now she's eating for one.

Jay Leno

So where did these cravings come from? I concluded it's the baby, _ordering in_. Prenatal takeout… If they get a hankering, they just pick up the umbilical cord and call.

Paul Reiser

The most common craving of pregnant women is not to be pregnant.

Phyllis Diller

Towards the end of my pregnancy, I was so huge. I'd sit in a chair positioned in front of the fridge, totally starkers with my massive belly. David used to pull me up from the chair, open the fridge so I could grab some food, then ease me back into the chair. He'd say, 'You look lovely, you know…'

Victoria Beckham

I gained so much weight when I had my last baby that when they wheeled me into the Delivery Room, the trolley got a flat tyre.

Phyllis Diller

Never go to your high school reunion pregnant or they will think that is all you have done since you graduated.

Erma Bombeck

—Mom drank when she was pregnant with us.
—Oh, Jackie, after a few months in Mom, we probably needed a shot or two.

Roseanne and Jackie, Roseanne

I'm drinking for two now.

Denise, The Royle Family

My wife had a lot of gas when she was pregnant with our first child. One night was particularly eventful so I said, 'Jan, would you mind going into another room until you're done?' She said, 'If I left the room every time I had to pass gas, I'd never be here.'

Dr Howard J. Bennett

I'm telling you: the fat ass, the farting – it's ridiculous…
And I have never been so horny in my entire life. That's
why you're supposed to be married when you're
pregnant as someone is obligated to have sex with you.

Miranda Hobbes, Sex and the City

Sometimes the foetus joined in and jived about a bit,
so it was like doing it with someone else in the room.

Michael Rosen, on sex during pregnancy

—Having sex with a pregnant woman is like putting
gas in a car you just wrecked.
—Well, luckily Peggy pulls into self-service.

Jefferson and Al Bundy, Married…With Children

I envy the kangaroo… The baby crawls out of the
womb when it is about two inches long, gets into
the pouch, and proceeds to mature. I'd have a baby
if it would develop in my handbag.

Rita Rudner

There comes a point when you can take no more
'ahhing' as in 'Ahh, you're pregnant', 'Ahh, how

you're glowing'. I always wanted to say, 'Yes, and so are my piles.'

Snowy, mumsnet.com

If pregnancy were a book they would cut the last two chapters.

Nora Ephron

The last two chapters: Giving birth

I feel like a man building a boat in his basement which he may not be able to get through the door. Trapped, frantic and trapped.

Abigail Lewis

With my first child I can recall screaming, 'Get this thing out of me! Get this thing out of me!' And that was the conception.

Joan Rivers

'Try nipple-stimulation to regulate labour,' the books suggest; so I spent 48 hours twiddling away at my nipples like some desperate old tart in a window in Amsterdam, to absolutely no effect.

Caitlin Moran

—People keep looking up me twinkle and I don't
know who they are!
—An ordinary day for you, then.

Dawn Swann and Carly Wicks, EastEnders

A male gynaecologist is like an auto mechanic who
never owned a car.

Carrie Snow

—What is a 'positive chandelier' sign?
—Well, that's when you manipulate the uterus with
the patient lying on the table, and it causes such
discomfort that they want to grab the chandelier if
you have one in your office.

Lawyer and Doctor

Death and taxes and childbirth! There's never any
convenient time for any of them.

Margaret Mitchell, Gone With the Wind

I told my mother I was going to have natural
childbirth. She said to me, 'Linda, you've been
taking drugs all your life. Why stop now?'

Linda Maldonado

If God wanted us to have a natural birth he would have put zippers on our stomachs.

Ruby Wax, How Do You Want Me?

I don't understand these women who want natural labour. To me it's like going to the dentist and asking for a natural root canal.

Ruby Wax, How Do You Want Me?

Next time I want the epidural at the moment of conception. Numb for nine months.

Heidi Joyce

I adopted and I had an epidural.

Rosie O'Donnell

I'm not interested in being Wonder Woman in the delivery room. Give me drugs.

Madonna

Dr Snow gave that blessed Chloroform and the effect was soothing, quieting and delightful beyond measure.

Queen Victoria, journal entry, 1853

Giving birth was easier than having a tattoo.

Nicole Appleton

Don't tell your kids you had an easy birth or they won't respect you. For years I used to wake up my daughter and say, 'Melissa, you ripped me to shreds. Now go back to sleep.'

Joan Rivers

Childbirth classes neglect to teach one critical skill: how to breathe, count and swear all at the same time.

Linda Fiterman

People are giving birth underwater now. They say it's less traumatic for the baby because it's underwater. But it's certainly more traumatic for the other people in the pool.

Elayne Boosler

I felt such a fool in the birthing pool in the middle of a hosepipe ban.

Victoria Wood

When I was giving birth, the nurse asked, 'Still think blondes have more fun?'

Joan Rivers

I felt like the whole country was in labour for me.

Diana, Princess of Wales

My mum was at the birth. She videoed it! Not the whole thing obviously, but she videoed me being stitched up. I remember looking up and her saying, 'Smile!'

Victoria Beckham

When my daughter was born, we videotaped the birth. Now when she makes me angry, I just hit rewind and put her back in.

Grace White

My friends want to show me films of their baby's birth. No, thank you, but I'll look at the video of the conception, if you have one.

Garry Shandling

If a guy films his wife giving birth, she ought to be able to film his haemorrhoid surgery later on: 'Look girls, Tony is totally dilated. What a trouper he was!'

Jeff Foxworthy

I well remember the totally ludicrous questions asked of me mere hours after I'd finally managed to heave the little darling out: 'Have you thought of contraception?' I was never sure whether this was a comment on my child or a genuine concern.

Lara, mumsnet.com

When the doctor is doing the episiotomy, just get the doctor to keep sewing, because you don't want anything going in there or coming out of there ever again.

Kathy Lette

I had a Jewish birth: they knock you out with the first pain; they wake you up when the hairdresser shows.

Joan Rivers

Cigars all round: Dads and birth

I asked my husband if he wanted to be in the room with me when I gave birth. He said, 'It would have to be a big room, and there would have to be a bar at one end.'

Rita Rudner

I told my wife I don't want to be there at the birth.
I didn't see why my evening should be ruined too.

Dennis Wolfberg

It's all any reasonable child can expect if the dad is
present at the conception.

Joe Orton

My husband didn't want to be there but I thought if
he was there when it went in, he can be there when
it comes out.

Kathy Lette

My wife, God bless her, was in labour for thirty-two
hours, and I was faithful to her the entire time.

Jonathan Katz

You have this myth, as the father, that if you're there
at the birth, you're sharing the birthing experience.
Unless you're opening an umbrella up your ass, I
don't think so.

Robin Williams

If men had to have babies they would only ever have one each.

Diana, Princess of Wales

They say that men can never experience the pain of childbirth. They can if you hit them in the goolies with a cricket bat for 14 hours.

Jo Brand

I remember the very first time I ever held my son in my arms as a newborn. Everything else in the universe melted away. There was just a father, a son, and the distant sound of my wife saying, 'If you ever come near me again, I'll drop you with a deer rifle.'

Frasier Crane, Frasier

My wife and I had all the complications you'd expect at a doctor's delivery – the epidural didn't work, they had to use forceps, and my mother-in-law stayed for three weeks.

Ryan James

Top ten similes for giving birth

GIVING BIRTH IS LIKE...

...taking your bottom lip and pulling it over your head.

Carol Burnett

...sitting on top of the Eiffel Tower and spinning.

Ruby Wax

...trying to push a grand piano through a transom.

Alice Roosevelt Longworth

...shitting a knife.

Angie Ostrowiski, Baby Mama

...a wet St Bernard coming in through the cat door.

Jeff Foxworthy

...watching two very inefficient removal men trying to get a very large sofa through a very small doorway, only in this case you can't say, 'Oh, sod it, bring it through the French windows.'

Victoria Wood

…being run over by a train.

Mother of Kate Llewellyn, The Dressmaker's Daughter

…getting out of your car through the exhaust pipe.

Murphy Brown, Murphy Brown

…shelling peas.

Helen Charge, giving birth to her sixth son after only
70 minutes in labour

…picking your nose. If you see someone else doing it, it's disgusting. But if you do it yourself, it's no big deal.

Joanne and Jeffrey Kimes

Look out for Mr Stork!

When they first brought the baby in to her she stared, inert, and thought, 'This is the author of my pain.'

Bessie Breuer

—Is it a boy or a girl?
—I think it's a bit early to start imposing roles on it, don't you?

New Mother and Obstetrician, Monty Python's
The Meaning of Life

Mary had a little lamb. The doctor was surprised.

Anon

Good work, Mary. We all knew you had it in you.

Dorothy Parker, congratulatory telegram to a friend

My obstetrician was so dumb that when I gave birth he forgot to cut the cord. For a year that kid followed me everywhere. It was like having a dog on a leash.

Joan Rivers

I was planning to eat my placenta, but wasn't sure how that squared with my vegetarianism, so settled for toast.

Victoria Wood

Giving birth is little more than a set of muscular contractions granting passage of a child. Then the mother is born.

Erma Bombeck

Bringing up baby

The easiest part of being a mother is giving birth – the hardest part of it is showing up every day thereafter.

Erma Bombeck

I remember leaving the hospital… thinking, 'Wait, are they going to let me just walk off with him? I don't know beans about babies! I don't have a licence to do this. We're just amateurs.'

Anne Tyler

Having a baby is like suddenly getting the world's worst roommate, like having Janis Joplin with a bad hangover and PMS come to stay with you.

Anne Lamott

I wonder why they say you have a baby. The baby has you.

Gallagher

Having a baby is like having an eight-pound to-do list. Every moment of the day is filled with something to feed, wipe, bathe or put down.

Kathleen Laccinole

I would like to have a bath one day soon, and maybe pee.

Sharon Stone

Motherhood changes you so that you forget you ever had time for small things like despising the colour pink.

Barbara Kingsolver

I used to be excellent. Now I have a baby and I couldn't tell you what day it is.

Gwyneth Paltrow

The first eight weeks are as tough as advertised – if I found time to wash, or make a phone call, I was doing well but in truth, I was so loved-up from the breast-feeding hormones I hardly cared. I felt as if I was on E.

Louise Wener

For about a month after my baby was born I bragged to everyone that I had the perfect baby because he never cried. Then I realised those baby monitors have volume control.

Frances Dilorinzo

One thing that made life easier for my generation was that one could put babies in prams outside in the garden for the whole morning; of course nobody does that now. And mothers are now afraid to let their children cry at all.

Dr Wendy Greengross

Some babies cry all night. This is known as colic. The only advantage of a baby having colic is that you don't have to keep checking to see if he is breathing.

Phyllis Diller

I was a closet pacifier advocate. So were most of my friends. Unknown to our mothers, we owned thirty or forty of those little suckers that were placed strategically around the house so a cry could be silenced in thirty seconds.

Erma Bombeck

My sister had a baby, and I went round to see her. She said, 'Do you want to wind him?' I said, 'I'll just give him a dead leg, shall I?'

Jimmy Carr

—You're really good about that no smoking in front of Baby David.
—Yeah I know, but I'm only doing it until he's old enough to be able to walk out the room himself and then it's up to him, innit?

Barbara and Denise, The Royle Family

I've always considered the real danger of smoking to be the chance of waking the kids when I go upstairs to get my cigarettes.

Phyllis Diller

—Omigod, the baby's put the condoms in his mouth!

—Oh, honey, relax. I have those in my mouth all the time.

Miranda Hobbes and Samantha Jones, Sex and the City

Why does everyone cheer when a child burps?

Peter Kay

The worst feature of a new baby is its mother's singing.

Kin Hubbard

—The doctor said that after you'd had the baby, you might feel that life wasn't worth living.

—I've felt that way for a long time, Frank.

Frank and Betty Spencer, Some Mothers Do 'Ave 'Em

She had post-natal depression. She showed me the baby… and then I had it as well.

Victoria Wood

A face only a mother could love

A new mother is pushing her pram through the park, taking her infant on her first outing. On the way she meets a neighbour, who coos over the baby. 'What a beautiful child!' she cries. The new mother smiles delightedly. 'That's nothing,' she brags, 'you should see her photograph!'

Anon

When I was born, my mother looked at me and looked at the afterbirth and screamed, 'Twins!'

Joan Rivers

I was so ugly when I was born, the doctor slapped my mother.

Henny Youngman

—It's a funny-looking baby. I've never seen one with a cleft chin and two warts under its nose.
—You're looking at the wrong end.
—No wonder it struggled when I tried to put the dummy in.

Cissie and Ada, aka Roy Barraclough and Les Dawson

No matter what the ordinary person says… no matter who it is that speaks, or what superlatives are employed, no baby is admired sufficiently to please the mother.

E.V. Lucas

If you desire to drain to the dregs the fullest cup of scorn and hatred that a fellow human being can pour out for you, let a young mother hear you call her baby 'it'.

Jerome K. Jerome

I have good-looking kids; thank goodness my wife cheats on me.

Rodney Dangerfield

Tom, Dick or Hannibal: Names

Naming our kid was a real trial. I seize up when I have to name a document on my computer.

Jeff Stilson

It gets harder to name children when you get older. Because by the time you're in your thirties every name you think of reminds you of someone you hate… We're down to Jethro and Nefertiti.

Rita Rudner

If we had a girl, my wife wanted to call her Sue. A lovely name, but which for Jews is generally a verb.

Dennis Wolfberg

Always end the name of your child with a vowel, so that when you yell the name will carry.

Bill Cosby

Christenings can be howling bad affairs, but of one which went off in a seemly and quiet way the mother explained afterwards that it was because 'my husband and I have been practising on him with a watering can for a whole week'.

Gerald Findler

One thing they never tell you about child raising is that for the rest of your life, at the drop of a hat, you are expected to know your child's name and how old he or she is.

Erma Bombeck

It sucks: Breastfeeding

Oh my God, I have milk coming out of my breasts. This is like having bacon come out of your elbow.

Murphy Brown, Murphy Brown

I can't get past the fact that *food* is coming out of my wife's breasts. What was once essentially an entertainment centre has now become a juice bar.

Paul Reiser

There are three reasons for breastfeeding: the milk is always at the right temperature; it comes in attractive containers; and the cat can't get it.

Irena Chalmers

Dad can nip off to the pub, but Mum is a 24-hour catering service – meals on heels.

Kathy Lette

I loved breastfeeding. I could just sit there and sink down into a novel. I got through the whole of Dickens while breastfeeding.

Alice Thomas Ellis

I breastfed for more than four years and this greatly enhanced my respect for cows.

Rachel Calcagno

My mother didn't breastfeed me. She said she just liked me as a friend.

Rodney Dangerfield

My baby's got a mouth like a staple-gun.

Breastfeeding Mother, ER

It hurts like a rhesus monkey biting your nipples.

Stefanie Wilder-Taylor

If the doctor thinks you ought to breastfeed and you don't want to, tell him you're a drug addict – you'd get the baby addicted too.

Katharine Whitehorn, How to Survive Children

I had a nightmare last night. I dreamed Dolly Parton was my mother and I was a bottle baby.

Henny Youngman

A child is too old to breastfeed when he can unhook mommy's bra with one hand.

Anthony Clark

Baby's first words

He used my body for nine months like it's an all-you-can-eat salad bar and his first word is 'Dada'.

Beth Cox, Rock Me Baby

Most children's first words are 'Mama' or 'Daddy'. Mine were, 'Do I have to use my own money?'

Erma Bombeck

My first words were 'Cadbury's Dairy Milk', and I didn't see the point of learning any words after that.

Victoria Wood

Only one thing is certain, it won't be 'Thank you'.

Jeff Green, The A–Z of Having a Baby

FAMOUS FIRST WORDS...

Paul Simon: Goodbye darkness, my old friend.

Lynn Roberts

Thomas Edison: I'm beginning to see the light…

Anon

Neil Armstrong: One small step for man…

Anon

Ethelred the Unready: No, honestly, I'm just fine in here.

Peter Veale

Tony Blair: Labour's over for me.

Anon

Jade Goody: Day One in the Big Brother World…

R. Jarski

Allan Sherman: Hello, Muddah. Hello, Faddah.

Marshall Karp

Bruce Forsyth: Nice to see you, to see you, nice!

R. Jarski

Jesus Christ: Merry Christmas!

James F. Daly

Buddha: Here we go again!

Brian Ruth

Brooklyn Beckham: Gucci, Gucci, goo.

Polly Stone

Joni Mitchell: I've looked at life from both sides now.

JoAnn Wexler

Stephen Fry: That's the last time I'm going up one of those.

Stephen Fry

Oedipus: I shall return!

Anon

Egon Ronay: *****

R. Jarski

Marie Stopes: Just sheer bloody irresponsibility.

A.G.D. McEvoy

Boris Karloff: I want my mummy!

Mrs Paul Stein

Yummy mummy or crummy mummy?

The three most beautiful sights – a potato garden in bloom, a ship in sail, and a woman after the birth of her baby.

Irish proverb

Motherhood brought many joys, but catching sight of the underneath of my neck in the mirror of the Tommee Tippee Activity Centre wasn't one of them.

Victoria Wood

My mother says I'm the reason she can't sit down. She blames me for the entire ruination of her body. This is a woman who attempted a tummy tuck in her eighth month of pregnancy.

Ruby Wax

—What do you want for Christmas?
—You can't wrap pelvic floors, can you?

Interviewer and Fay Ripley, actress and new mother

Think of stretch marks as pregnancy service stripes.

Joyce Armor

My boyfriend commented on the size of my Caesarean scar, and then I had to say, 'No, it isn't one. It's just that this slip's too tight.'

Helen Lederer

I've got my figure back after giving birth. Sad, I'd hoped to get somebody else's.

Caroline Quentin

Celebrity mommies say, 'I didn't get my figure back straight away – it did take about twenty minutes.'

Real mommies carry their stomachs up to bed over one arm.

Victoria Wood

I'm happy to say I lost the weight after the baby. Of course, it took me four years, and we adopted.

Andrea Henry

The funniest thing about motherhood is how you let yourself go. I look in the mirror, and I think, Oh, my God, I've had that moustache for three weeks! I have to cut it. I even have three long black hairs that grow out of my cheek.

Jenny McCarthy, model

Keep smiling and don't worry about your hair. It will be full of baby sick for months.

Anna Friel, actress

Kids are cute, but they got that honesty thing and there's no need for that. I'm in the bathroom taking a shower and my daughter walks in. 'Gosh, Mom, I hope that when I grow up my breasts will be nice and long like yours.'

Roseanne

If anything could be less desirable than bloated, humongous 'mummy bags', it's a deflated pair... Not unlike a tyre with a slow puncture, they will gradually diminish and I will...be left with what can be described only as two ping-pong balls in bin liners.

Ulrika Jonsson

I'm thirty-five. I've had three children. I can hide a can of cat food under each breast.

Grace Kelly, Grace Under Fire

> See the mothers in the park,
> Ugly creatures chiefly;
> Someone must have loved them once—
> in the dark and briefly.

Anon

There are only two things a child will share willingly – communicable diseases and his mother's age.

Dr Benjamin Spock

As long as a woman can look ten years younger than her own daughter, she is perfectly satisfied.

Oscar Wilde

—Should I have surgery? Darling, look at mama.
—Yes. Get your mouth sewn up!

Edina and Saffy Monsoon, Absolutely Fabulous

—How would you feel if I used your child support payments for plastic surgery?
—Mom, you look fine.
—If you could cut back to two meals a day I could get a chemical peel.

Susan and Julie Mayer, Desperate Housewives

Curly, dimpled lunatic: Child-rearing

We all of us wanted babies – but did any of us want children?

Eda J. LeShan

A child is a curly, dimpled lunatic.

Ralph Waldo Emerson

Having children gives your life a purpose. Right now, my purpose is to get some sleep.

Reno Goodale

Hang your kids' pyjamas in sight. It keeps your spirits up through the day.

Phyllis Diller

The art of being a parent is to sleep while the baby isn't looking.

Anon

Adam and Eve had many advantages, but the principal one was that they escaped teething.

Mark Twain

The twos aren't always terrible. Even if they are, take heart, as kids aged three to six generally believe their parents are the most amazing beings alive and wish to be exactly like them. How scary is that?

Anon

Useful Things For a Parent to Know: Who holds the record for the highest number of goals scored for England; the name of the most poisonous snake in the world; what God looks like; whether the Queen is allowed to eat sweets before dinner; that the answer to 'Are you making a mess in there, Stephen?' is always 'Yes'; that the answer to 'Are you going to get down off there, Natasha?' is always 'No'.

Laurie Graham, Parents' Survival Guide

I am sure there is no mother this side of a mental institution that refuses to treat her children to a baby-sitter. Once the sitters tried to up their prices, but I was firm. Three dollars an hour and they supply their own ammunition.

Phyllis Diller

I offered one baby-sitter a magazine to read and she said, 'No thanks, I'd rather just poke through the drawers.'

Phyllis Diller

None of the kids cried when we left the house, but we often had baby-sitters that did.

Phyllis Diller

Birthday parties make you realise the luckiest people in the world are those with children born on February 29.

Phyllis Diller

'Won't it be wonderful,' my husband said as we recovered from a four-year-old's party, 'when they're teenagers and it's just pot and sexual intercourse and we don't have to do *anything*?'

Katharine Whitehorn, How to Survive Children

The main purpose of children's parties is to remind you that there are children more awful than your own.

Katharine Whitehorn, How to Survive Children

The next time you have to go to a boring kiddie activity, invite another mom-friend along. Hide Chardonnay in two sippy cups for the two of you to nurse undercover.

Melina Gerosa Bellows

My son is into this nose-picking thing. The least he can do is act like an adult: buy a car and sit in traffic.

Roseanne

The real menace in dealing with a five-year-old is that in no time at all you begin to sound like a five-year-old.

Jean Kerr

I don't think my six children had a deprived childhood, exactly, but I think I had a deprived motherhood.

Alice Thomas Ellis

Don't drink until the children are in bed. We made this rule once, but they got so sick of getting tucked in at 4.30pm.

Phyllis Diller

It is not advisable to put your head around your child's door to see if it is asleep. It was.

Faith Hines

My twins are finally sleeping through the night.
Well, I don't know if they are, but I am.

Kerri Louise

Good night, sleep tight, don't let the bed bugs bite!

Anon

No, it's not that Spock! Expert advice

The biggest problem facing a pregnant woman is
not nausea or fatigue or her wardrobe – it's free
advice.

Sophia Loren

They caution pregnant women not to drink alcohol.
It may harm the baby. I think that's ironic. If it
wasn't for alcohol most women wouldn't be that way.

Rita Rudner

I will never forget [Doctor Spock's] stern advice on
how to stop a toddler getting out of its cot several

times a night. He counselled the child's sleep-deprived parents to throw a badminton net over the cot, tie it securely at each corner and to close their ears to the child's screams. Such harsh pragmatism could have come straight from the Ann Widdecombe Book of Kiddie Care.

Sue Townsend, Public Confessions of a Middle-Aged Woman

I'd completely lost my bearings trying to follow potty training instructions from a psychiatric expert who guaranteed success with his methods in three efficient days. I was stuck on step one, which stated without an atom of irony: 'Before you begin, remove all stubbornness from the child.'

Mary Kay Blakely

Don't never read any of the books by experts. They don't never have kids neither. They say things like, 'Don't ever hit your kids in anger.' Think about that. When would be a good time to hit them? When you're feeling festive?

Roseanne

'Bathe your child with language' says [child-rearing expert] Mia Kellmer Pringle, and some of the language I've bathed mine with would make the soap blush.

Katharine Whitehorn, How to Survive Children

The more people have studied different methods of bringing up children the more they have come to the conclusion that what good mothers and fathers instinctively feel like doing for their babies is the best after all.

Dr Benjamin Spock

A little girl goes into her local library and picks up a book called *Advice For Young Mothers*. 'Why do you want a book like that?' asks the librarian. The little girl replies, 'Because I collect moths.'

Anon

Training a baby by the book is a good idea, only you need a different book for each baby.

Dan Bennett

Motherhood is like Albania – you can't trust the description in the books, you have to go there.

Marni Jackson

I tried my best but there are no schools for mums. You learn by your mistakes.

Sharon Osbourne

The only thing you have to remember about babies is not to stick your thumb in that soft bit on their heads.

Linda Smith

And whatever you do, don't store your child's winter jacket in the attic while he's wearing it.

Phyllis Diller

On the job: Day-to-day mothering

Every day I start out Mary Poppins but I end up Cruella de Vil.

Deborah, Mum's the Word

For me, parenting is like dieting. Every day, I wake up filled with resolve and good intentions, perfection in view, and every day I somehow stray from the path. The difference is, with dieting I usually make it to lunch.

Marion Winik, The Lunch-Box Chronicles

Alligators have the right idea. They eat their young.

Ida Corwin, Mildred Pierce

It's not easy being a mother. If it were, fathers would do it.

Dorothy Zbornak, The Golden Girls

Running General Motors or breaking stones would have offered an easier option than looking after children.

Alice Thomas Ellis

When my husband comes home, if the kids are still alive, I figure I've done my job.

Roseanne

The story of a mother's life: trapped between a scream and a hug.

Cathy Guisewite

I know how to do anything – I'm a mom.

Roseanne

A woman can do _anything_, but not _everything_.
Consequently, the wise woman shares the tasks and
the credit, if any, with family, friends and colleagues.

June E. Gabler

To be effective and to gain the respect she needs to
function, a mother must have her children believe
she has never engaged in sex, never made a bad
decision, never caused her own mother a moment's
anxiety, and was never a child.

Erma Bombeck

Any mother could perform the job of several air-
controllers with ease.

Lisa Alther

A mother always has to think twice, once for herself
and once for her child.

Sophia Loren

Parenthood is not what you ought to do; it's what you can stand.

Katharine Whitehorn, How to Survive Children

The world's worst mother: Guilty secrets

Some mornings when I am desperate for more sleep, I lie to my husband about how many times I got up in the night with the baby.

Mum's the Word

One time I left the grocery store without my kids. I just forgot them. The manager found them in the frozen food aisle, eating Eskimo Pies.

Anonymous mother

A friend spooned Calamine lotion into her toddler late one night, thinking it was Pepto Bismol – 'Can you believe it? If he hadn't gagged, I might have poisoned him.'

Mary Kay Blakely

—Vicky, where's your baby?

—Swapped it for a Westlife CD.

—How could you do such a thing?

—I know, they're rubbish.

Social Worker and Vicky Pollard, Little Britain

Oh, honey, you're not the world's worst mother.
What about the freezer lady in Georgia?

Homer Simpson

Every time I do something bad, I just say to my kids,
'Save it for the book!'

Rosie O'Donnell

I find it much easier to be a good mum in public.

Mum's the Word

Of course I don't always enjoy being a mother.
At those times my husband and I hole up
somewhere in the wine country, eat, drink, make
mad love and pretend we were born sterile and
raise poodles.

Dorothy DeBolt, mother of 8 and adoptive mother of 14

Queen of worriers

Anna and Rachel meet for the first time in 50 years. Anna starts to talk about her children: 'My son is a doctor, and my daughter is married with two children. So, Rachel, tell me about yours.' 'Unfortunately, we never had any children,' says Rachel. 'No children? Then tell me, what do you do for aggravation?'

Anon

If you don't have children the longing for them will kill you, and if you do, the worrying over them will kill you.

Buchi Emecheta

Every minute in the presence of a child takes seven minutes off your life.

Barbara Kingsolver

One day, my son had a friend over for a play date after school… While the kids were snacking on some of my homemade brownies, I heard my son question

74

his friends, 'What are you so worried about?
Whatever it is, well, you can tell my mother and she
will worry for you. She is the Queen of Worriers.'

Judy Klau Pace

My mother was the Jewish Lourdes. People always
came to her with their problems.

Sammy Cahn

I used to be a reasonably careless and adventurous
person before I had children; now I am morbidly
obsessed by seat-belts and constantly afraid that low-
flying aircraft will drop on my children's school.

Margaret Drabble

Mothers had a thousand thoughts to get through
within a day, and… most of those were about
avoiding disaster.

Natalie Kusz

I was very overprotected as a child. My tricycle had
seven wheels. And a driver.

Rita Rudner

—How do you feel that your mum's so worried about your addiction?

—If I was a teetotal vicar somewhere she'd probably be equally worried that my bicycle-clips were too tight.

Pete Doherty, pop star, and Kirsty Wark, Newsnight

Your children tell you casually years later what it would have killed you with worry to know at the time.

Mignon McLaughlin

The central struggle of parenthood is to let our hopes for our children outweigh our fears.

Ellen Goodman

You get a lot of tension. You get a lot of headaches. I do what it says on the aspirin bottle: take two and keep away from children.

Roseanne

Father, dear Father

The place of the father in the modern suburban
family is a very small one, particularly if he plays golf.

Bertrand Russell

Common sense tells us a father's role is not equal to a
mother's. A man can become a father and not know.

Germaine Greer

Mothers are a biological necessity; fathers are a social
invention.

Margaret Mead

Whoever heard of Father Earth?

Vance Bourjaily

—Yeah, sure, for you, Lisa, a baby's all fun and games.
For me, it's diaper changes and midnight feedings.
—Doesn't Mom do all that stuff?
—Yeah, but I have to hear about it.

Homer and Lisa Simpson

A woman knows everything about her children. She knows about dental appointments and football games and best friends and favourite foods and romances and secret fears and hopes and dreams. A man is vaguely aware of some short people living in the house.

Dave Barry

You tell me who has to leave the office when the kid bumps his head or slips on a milk carton.

Wendy Wasserstein

The thing to remember about fathers is, they're men.

Phyllis McGinley

Things a Father Should Know: how to cook a meal the children will eat; how to say 'That's final' and not go back on it as soon as his wife's out of sight; that Elizabethandthechildren is actually four words, not one.

Katharine Whitehorn, How to Survive Children

A good father is a little bit of mother.

Lee Salk

A father had to work only half as hard as any mother to be considered twice as good.

Mary Kay Blakely

Babies don't need fathers, but mothers do. Someone who is taking care of a baby needs to be taken care of.

Amy Heckerling

Having children accentuates more marital faults than adultery does.

Julie Burchill

—Daddy, who is the boss between you and mommy?
—Who is the boss? You have to ask that?! *I'm* the boss. Mommy is only the decision maker.

Max and Lenny Weinrib, Mighty Aphrodite

My father wore the trousers in the family – at least, after the court order.

Vernon Chapman

Not now, honey, Mommy's threatening Daddy.

Lynette Scavo, to her young son, Desperate Housewives

Marge, can I go out and play?

Homer Simspon

Pooperman: Toilet training

In the eyes of a mother, there is one single determining factor as to whether her husband is a good father or not: does he change the baby's nappy?

Anon

Any mother with half a skull knows that when Daddy's little boy becomes Mommy's little boy, the kid is so wet he's treading water.

Erma Bombeck

Like many other women, I could not understand why every man who changed a diaper has felt compelled to write a book about it.

Barbara Ehrenreich

I went right off that Frankie Dettori when I found out he didn't do nappies.

Peter Kay

Things a Father Should Know: how to change a
nappy – *and* dispose of the old one.

Katharine Whitehorn, How to Survive Children

Changing a diaper is a lot like getting a present from
your grandmother – you're not sure what you've got
but you're pretty sure you're not going to like it.

Jeff Foxworthy

'Does my bum look big in this?' I'm afraid so.

Jeff Green, The A–Z of Having a Baby

I don't have any problem with nappies because I
have never changed one.

Madonna

When he's two, go out and buy a pot, two dozen
pairs of knickers, a sponge for the puddles, and a
large bag of treacle toffees. The toffees are for keeping
your mouth busy when you might otherwise feel like
saying something.

Laurie Graham, Parents' Survival Guide

I did hear of one father wondering if his daughter would be the only girl to go straight from nappies to Tampax.

Katharine Whitehorn, How to Survive Children

You've lost that loving feeling: Sex

Amnesia: the condition that enables a woman who has gone through labour to have sex again.

Joyce Armor

I could have been sexually abused, but after I was born my parents were hardly interested in having sex with each other.

P.J. O'Rourke

People have babies because they secretly long for celibacy.

Cathy Crimmins

You can't have a sex life in a nursing bra.

Mum's the Word

When my old man wanted sex, my mother would show him a picture of me.

Rodney Dangerfield

Kids are a contraceptive. Every time you are in the mood to make love, the baby wakes up or the toddler toddles in. Parents only need one sex tip: Vaseline – on the doorknobs.

Kathy Lette

—Mommy, what was that?
—It's an electrical ear cleaner!
—It was kind of big…

Taylor and Karen Buckman, Parenthood

Real mothers think sex is like full-time employment: it's a nice idea but it'll never happen again in their lifetime.

Victoria Wood

I'm fine about sex. Just don't wake me.

Anon

Birth control

I had a baby in 1988, which proved my theory that stretch pants alone do not make an effective contraceptive.

Victoria Wood

I'm Catholic. When my mother found my diaphragm, I had to tell her it was a bathing cap for my cat.

Lizz Winstead

—The diaphragm is a pain in the ass.
—You're putting it in the wrong place!

Carole Montgomery and Friend

My period was late, and I had nothing to worry about, but I worried anyway: 'Maybe I am going to have the Lord's child.'

Penelope Lombard

Even the best birth control method is only effective 99 out of 100 times. I can't beat those odds!

Roz Doyle, Frasier

My friend spent fifty quid on a baby alarm and still got pregnant.

Linda Smith

A friend of mine confused her Valium with her birth control pills. She had 14 kids but didn't give a shit.

Joan Rivers

Giving away baby clothes and nursery furniture is a major cause of pregnancy.

Esther Selsdon

Me and my husband just found a foolproof method of birth control. Every night before we go to bed, we spend an hour with our kids.

Roseanne

Feeling broody... again

There was an old lady who lived in a shoe, she had so many children she didn't know what to do – obviously.

I'm Sorry I Haven't a Clue

—I have twenty children.

—Why do you have so many?

—I like children.

—I like my cigar, but I take it out of my mouth now and again.

Contestant and Groucho Marx, You Bet Your Life

I've been married 14 years and I have three kids. Obviously, I breed well in captivity.

Roseanne

I came from a big family. As a matter of fact, I never got to sleep alone until I got married.

Lewis Grizzard

I planned on having one husband and seven children, but it turned out the other way around.

Lana Turner

Reinhardt was never his mother's favourite – and he was an only child.

Thomas Berger

An advantage to having one child is you always know who did it.

Babs Bell Hajdusiewicz

I've got two wonderful children – and two out of five ain't bad.

Henny Youngman

The great advantage of living in a large family is that early lesson of life's essential unfairness.

Nancy Mitford

—You know Lorraine across the road… she's been sterilised. Well, four's enough for any single mother.
—I bet it's like a clown's pocket down there.

Barbara and Jim, The Royle Family

Never have more children than you have car windows.

Erma Bombeck

When your first baby drops her dummy, you sterilise it. When your second baby drops her dummy, you tell the dog: 'Fetch.'

Bruce Lansky

We went all out with new things for our first child and the second one had nothing but hand-me-downs. The bronzed baby shoes almost killed him.

Phyllis Diller

We were very tense when Kevin was little. It's because he was our first. If he got a scratch we were hysterical. By the third kid, you let 'em juggle knives.

Karen Buckman, Parenthood

I got more children than I can rightly take care of, but I ain't got more than I can love.

Ossie Guffy

Happy families

See our family. And feel better about yours.

Tagline, The Simpsons Movie

Sharon is the organiser, the governor, she organises us all 'cause I'm clueless. I get up in the morning, I've got a drawer full of black underpants, and I go, 'Which ones should I wear?' They're all black, you know?

Ozzy Osbourne

It's like living with homeless people. They're cute but they just chase you around all day long going, 'Can I have a dollar? I'm missing a shoe! I need a ride!'

Kathleen Madigan

I'm at the stage of motherhood where I'm putting the kids under sink and the lethal household substances within reach.

Kathy Lette

The informality of family life is a blessed condition that allows us to become our best while looking our worst.

Marge Kennedy

When our daughter was seven we were discussing 'in-laws'. After explaining how Mummy's mother was my mother-in-law, I gave her a little test and said: 'When you are grown up and have your own husband, what will I be?' Her response was, 'Dead.' I was then 55.

Ian Sheratte

Why do grandparents and grandchildren get on so well? They have the same enemy – the mother.

Claudette Colbert

Our kid's keeping our marriage together. Neither of us want custody.

Phyllis Diller

—Sometimes I think we're the worst family in town.
—Maybe we should move to a larger community.

Homer and Marge Simpson

—If my mother and father move here, I'm gonna be sleeping on a bunk for the rest of my life, because I'm gonna be in prison for blowing 'em away!
—Honey, honey, be realistic. You don't know how to use a gun. I'll do it.

Roseanne and Dan Conner, Roseanne

Happiness is having a large, loving, caring, close-knit family – in another city.

George Burns

Going it alone: Single mum

Wayne, I want us to split up. I'm the only mum on
the estate with a live-in partner… I should be a
single mother by now, it's embarrassing for the kids.
They get teased by the others, 'You've got a daddy!
You've got a daddy!'

Waynetta Slob, Harry Enfield and Chums

Why don't you get some Chinese food for dinner?
I've left your father. Love, Mom.

Pat Gibbs, a note to her son, Valentino Returns

—She says she wants a divorce.
—What? Just because she caught him flirting with a
couple of nurses?
—She was giving birth at the time.

Ken and Joe, Early Doors

Yes, single-parent families are different from two-parent families. And urban families are different from rural ones, and families with six kids and a dog are different from one-child, no-pet households, but even if there is only one adult presiding at the dinner table, yours is every bit as much a real family as are the Waltons.

Marge Kennedy

The worst thing that's happened in this country in the last twenty years is the use of language to deceive. We say things like single-parent families when it's really single-mother families.

Fran Lebowitz

For many divorced women, the real challenge begins once they find a man to date.

Claudia Bowe

As someone with virtually no interest in the 'mom' part of you, he's the perfect antidote for all those years you've spent feeling like nothing *but* a mom.

Joyce Maynard, on dating after divorce

Another good thing about going to parties alone: no one assumes that an adequate conversation opener is to ask what your husband does.

Ann P. Harris

The prospect of removing my clothing in front of a new partner appals me… I can look pretty good with my clothes on; but, after two children, lingerie is now less a case of bodily adornment than of shoring up the landslides.

Lowri Turner

I tell younger men, 'I could be your mum.' And they say, 'But you're not.' Yahoo!

Sharon Stone

She's Doing Everything She Told her Daughter Not to Do.

Tagline, Sex & the Single Mom

Mom, There's a Man in the Kitchen and he's Wearing Your Robe: The Single Mom's Guide to Dating Well Without Parenting Poorly

Ellie Slott Fisher, book title

I think Marc found it difficult being with a woman with kids… Johnny was going through potty training and would come in three times a night to wake us up, then at 6am he'd hurl his nappy over my head. I'm his mum and didn't mind one bit. Marc was a gentleman and didn't say anything – but it must have been a shock for him.

Cerys Matthews, on why her 'post-jungle' romance
with Marc Bannerman ended

Men may come and men may go, but the one constant in life for a single mother is her children.

Joyce Maynard

The real killer was when you married the wrong person but had the right children.

Ann Beattie

—Tell me again why I fought for custody of you?
—You were using me to hurt Dad.
—Oh, that's right. Oh God.

Susan and Julie Mayer, Desperate Housewives

According to an article in *USA Today*, children from single-parent homes have much better verbal skills than children from two-parent homes. However, children from two-parent homes are far superior at bitterly sarcastic repartee.

Dennis Miller

That's the only good thing about divorce. You get to sleep with your mother.

Little Mary, The Women

There's nothing to do! Fun with Mum

I had the most satisfactory of childhoods because Mother, small, delicate-boned, witty and articulate, turned out to be exactly my age.

Kay Boyle

Never play peek-a-boo with a child on a long plane trip. There's no end to the game. Finally I grabbed him by the bib and said, 'Look. It's always gonna be me.'

Rita Rudner

Do not, on a rainy day, ask your child what he feels like doing because I assure you that what he feels like doing, you won't feel like watching.

Fran Lebowitz

Children make the most desirable opponents in Scrabble as they are both easy to beat and fun to cheat.

Fran Lebowitz

Notoriously insensitive to subtle shifts in mood, children will persist in discussing the colour of a recently sighted cement-mixer long after one's own interest in the topic has waned.

Fran Lebowitz

—Mom, why do you always find ways to amuse yourself at my expense?
—Because we don't have cable and I can't crochet.

Dorothy Zbornak and Sophia Petrillo, The Golden Girls

Children only want high-technology toys nowadays. My son has an imaginary playmate that requires batteries.

Anon

—[*Bart is playing a video game*] How could you kill your own mother?
— It was just a game. A game I was enjoying until you mommed all over it.

Marge and Bart Simspon

You can always tell non-parents by the type of gift they buy for your kids. We had a single friend…who took it upon himself to surprise our kids with a present. It was a bright green gooey toy called Gak. I wish I was still punching him.

Ray Romano

One of the disadvantages of enrolling your daughters in dance class is that eventually they put on a recital you have to attend.

Bruce Lansky

If you must give your child lessons, send him to driving school. He is far more likely to end up owning a Datsun than he is a Stradivarius.

Fran Lebowitz

I have new-age friends in California who try to do that politically correct kind of stuff and so they gave their little girl a toolbox of plastic tools. They were horrified later that night when they came into her room and found her putting the hammer to bed.

Rob Becker

There's no such thing as fun for the whole family; there are no massage parlours with ice cream and jewellery.

Jerry Seinfeld

Keeping the children occupied is an entirely modern headache – in the good old days one used the children to mind goats or sweep floors; that long summer holiday, at the end of which, as one woman put it, 'the only creative play we could think of was to send them out into the garden with spades to dig graves', was originally designed for harvesting – I just wish they'd revive it.

Katharine Whitehorn, How to Survive Children

No matter what the critics say, it's hard to believe that a television programme which keeps four children quiet for an hour can be all bad.

Beryl Pfizer

Remember, it is easier to turn television sets louder than it is to turn kids lower.

Phyllis Diller

Time spent with your family doing ordinary things is the most extraordinary time of all.

Jan Blaustone

Burnt toast and a bunch of daffs: Mother's Day

Don't forget Mother's Day. Or as they call it in Beverly Hills, Dad's Third Wife Day.

Jay Leno

Mother's Day is the day we honour the woman we blame for all our personal problems.

David Letterman

This country devotes one day of the year to mothers, and an entire week to pickles.

Anon

I appreciate the chance to visit my mom on Mother's Day – it's like taking a refresher course in guilt.

Woody Allen

No man would dare say a bad word against Mother's Day in public; or a good word for it in private.

Alistair Cooke

Mother's Day and Father's Day are alike, except that on Father's Day you can get away with buying a cheaper gift.

Susan Brown

Mothers make a list of things they want for Mother's Day, summon their children, and say, 'Go see your father, get some money from him, and surprise me with some of these.' The kids go to the father and say, 'Dad, we need $8,000 for some presents for Mom.'

Bill Cosby

When I was six I made my mother a little hat – out of her new blouse.

Lilly Daché

The biggest surprise my family could give me on Mother's Day would be to remember it.

Kathy Lette

When you feel neglected, think of the female salmon who lays 3 million eggs but no one remembers her on Mother's Day.

Sam Ewing

Nine months' pregnancy, many agonising hours in labour, a cleavage that will never be perky again and all we get is some burned toast. Then someone will be unable to find their car keys/skate-board/Bratz doll and it will be back to business as usual.

Lowri Turner

I told my mother on Mother's Day, 'Mum, you've been bending over that hot stove all your life. Straighten up!'

Anon

There will be other Mother's Days and a parade of gifts that will astound and amaze you, but not one of them will ever measure up to the sound of your children on Mother's Day whispering, 'Don't you dare bleed on Mom's breakfast.'

Erma Bombeck

I did it my way: Mothering styles

Mom is Many Things. Normal Isn't One of Them.

Tagline, Mermaids

My mum – a strange creature from the time when pickles on toothpicks were still the height of sophistication.

Bridget Jones, Bridget Jones's Diary

Good old Jeremy's mum, the more sophisticated end of the mum spectrum; the sort of mum you'd buy in John Lewis.

Mark Corrigan, Peep Show

Olive oil? Asparagus? If your mother wasn't so fancy, we could just shop at the gas station like normal people.

Homer Simpson

—What's Steve's mother like?
—Imagine Steve…in a wig…drunk.

Carrie Bradshaw and Miranda Hobbes, Sex and the City

The difference between hockey moms and pit bulls? Lipstick.

Sarah Palin, US vice presidential candidate

By 7am Sarah Palin would have already had a baby, disembowelled a moose, jogged six miles, electrified the free world and had sex with her husband. I am a complete waste of space and a sorry excuse for a wife, mother and woman.

Rachel Johnson

My mother should have raised cobras, not children!

Tom Wingo, The Prince of Tides

My childhood was pretty bad. When I was seven, my mother told me I was selfish. One day I asked for dinner. 'You're just like your father,' she said.

Gloria Brinkworth

I had one of those mothers who was always telling people her daughter was her best friend. When she said it, I'd think, 'Great, not only do I have a shitty mother, my best friend's a loser bitch.'

Dedee Truitt, The Opposite of Sex

Mother was the real-life Wicked Witch of the West.

Judy Garland

There was no love in my home. I was one of 15 children, and the only contact I had with my mother was when she took me between her knees to pull lice out of my head.

Charles Bronson

Growing up, my mom always claimed to feel bad when a bird would slam head first into our living

room window. If she *really* felt bad, though, she'd
have moved the bird feeder outside.

Rich Johnson

—The bank robber took your mother hostage!
—Oh my god! That poor man!

Val Toriello and Fran Fine, The Nanny

I was talking to my son the other day, and he said
that his friend Billy has two mommies. I thought,
wow! Billy's daddy is a lucky guy. My wife would
never go for that.

Brian Kiley

—I've got a kid. He's being raised by two women at
the moment.
—Oh, y'know, I mean that works… You don't need
a male. Two mothers are fine.
—Really? Because I always feel very few people
survive one mother.

Mary Wilkie and Isaac Davis, Manhattan

My mother buried three husbands – and two of
them were only napping.

Rita Rudner

I had my mother on our Mother's Day show... and I could not hug her. Oprah Winfrey who hugs everyone could not hug her own mother. But we have never hugged, we have never said, 'I love you.' And yet we are both at peace with that.

Oprah Winfrey

I'm never going to write my autobiography and it's all my mother's fault. I didn't hate her, so I have practically no material.

Jean Kerr

My mother was a wit, but never a sentimental one. Once, when somebody in our house stepped on our cat's paw, she turned to the cat and said sternly, 'I told you not to go around barefoot!'

Zero Mostel

If Kerry Katona is celebrity mum of the year again, I'm going to vote Abi Titmuss as most inspirational virgin.

Anonymous mother

Of course, the trouble with my mother is that she never had any children…

Overheard on a bus

I think the way to judge a mother is by her children.

Barbara Bush, mother of President George W. Bush

There was no way to be a perfect mother and a million ways to be a good one.

Jill Churchill

Having it all: Working mothers

I love my husband. I love my children. But I want something more. Like a life.

Roseanne

Being asked to decide between your passion for work and your passion for children was like being asked by your doctor whether you preferred him to remove your brain or your heart.

Mary Kay Blakely

—How can you be both a lawmaker and a mother?
—I have a brain and a uterus, and I use both.

Pat Schroeder, US congresswoman

I can't have a baby. I have a 12:30 lunch meeting!

J.C. Wiatt, Baby Boom

Why not have your first baby at 60, when your husband is already dead and your career is over? Then you can really devote yourself to it.

Fran Lebowitz

—It's not the same for men. Charlie Chaplin had babies when he was 73.
—Yeah, but he was too old to pick them up.

Sally and Harry, When Harry Met Sally

By the time my parents had me, they were old. My mother had labour pains and hot flushes.

Marietta Daniel

I want to spend more time with my family, but I'm not sure they want to spend more time with me.

Esther Rantzen

I thought my mom's whole purpose was to be my mom. That's how she made me feel.

Natasha Gregson Wagner, daughter of Natalie Wood

My mother was a normal mother, just like anybody's. She cooked, cleaned, kissed us goodnight, and weekends, was an Elvis impersonator.

Larry the Cable Guy

Like most people I lived for a long time with my mother and father. My father liked to watch the wrestling. My mother liked to wrestle.

Jeanette Winterson, Oranges Are Not The Only Fruit

My mom was a ventriloquist, and she was always throwing her voice. For ten years I thought the dog was telling me to kill my father.

Wendy Liebman

My mum was a lollipop lady – by which I mean she had a very thin body and a big, round, red, sticky head.

Harry Hill

It's weird that I have a parent who's a shrink. It's hard to think of my mom solving other people's problems when she's the root of all mine.

Carol Leifer

When you have children, you have to stop being the picture and become the frame. Now, because of what I do, I hate the feeling that my children might feel I'm the picture.

Nigella Lawson, Domestic Goddess and TV chef

To talk to a child, to fascinate him, is much more difficult than to win an electoral victory. But it is more rewarding.

Colette

The truth is, women can Have It All, but Not All At Once. It's important to remember that perfect mums only exist in American sitcoms.

Kathy Lette

A man at his desk in a room with a closed door is a man at work. A woman at a desk in any room is available.

Marya Mannes

I think we're seeing in working mothers a change from 'Thank God it's Friday' to 'Thank God it's Monday'. If any working mother has not experienced that feeling, her children are not adolescent.

Ann Diehl

Every mother is a working mother.

Anon

Sweet mother of mercy: Religion

God could not be everywhere, and therefore he made mothers.

Jewish saying

My mother is Jewish, my father Catholic. When I went to confession, I'd pray, 'Bless me, father, for I have sinned, and I think you know my lawyer, Mr Cohen.'

Bill Maher

An ounce of mother is worth a pound of clergy.

Spanish proverb

When I was a kid my mother switched religions from Catholic to Episcopalian. Which is what, Catholic Lite? One-third less guilt than regular religion.

Rick Corso

The Wise Men came to see the infant Jesus, and they enthused over his beauty. But his mother, Mary, was disconsolate. 'What's the matter?' they asked. 'I did so want a girl,' she said.

Groucho Marx

Jesus was a Jew, yes, but only on his mother's side.

Archie Bunker, All in the Family

Men made God in their image, and he's a deadbeat dad. Never sends money, doesn't come to visit, can't get him on the phone.

Mimi Gonzalez

I was recently born again. I must admit it's a glorious and wonderful experience. I can't say my mother enjoyed it a whole lot.

John Wing

My Yiddishe mama

My mother is a typical Jewish mother. They sent her home from jury duty – she insisted she was guilty.

Cathy Ladman

A Jewish mother is an eternal pain and an eternal blessing.

Laurie Rozakis

I always wanted to do comedy, but my mother was not in favour of it. She used to wake me up in the middle of the night... 'Vy don't you get a job? Vy don't you become a lawyer, an accountant? Do something! Become a doctor. Vy do you have to become an actor and make yourself crazy?' Mom, why do you talk to me like that? We're not even Jewish.

Harvey Korman

All mothers are Jewish mothers.

Mother of Philip Roth, author

Top ten Jewish mother jokes

A proud Jewish mother is taking her two small boys for a walk when she meets an old friend of the family. 'Goodness, how your children are growing up,' the friend exclaims. 'How old are they now?' 'Well,' says the mother, 'the doctor is seven and the lawyer is five.'

—How many Jewish mothers does it take to change a light bulb?

—[*sigh*] Don't bother. I'll just sit here in the dark. I don't want to be a nuisance to anyone.

A Jewish boy comes home from school and tells his mother he's been given a part in the school play. 'Wonderful. What part is it?' The boy says, 'I play the part of the Jewish husband.' The mother scowls and says, 'Go back and tell the teacher you want a speaking part.'

A mother gave her son two ties as a going-away present when he left home to go to college. When he returned home for the holidays, he wore one of the ties to show his appreciation of the gift. His mother took one look at the tie and enquired anxiously, 'What's the matter? The other one you didn't like?'

A Yiddishe mama is strolling in the park at dusk. Suddenly, from behind the bushes, a strange man jumps out, opens his raincoat and flashes her. Unruffled, she takes a look, shakes her head and says, 'Call that a lining?'

—Mama, great news! I got married!

—How wonderful, darling!

—Mama, I might as well tell you… he's not Jewish. Also, he doesn't have a job…and we have no place to live.

—Don't worry, darling, you'll come and live with me!

—But, Mama, you only have one bedroom. Where will you sleep?

—Oh, don't worry about me. The minute I hang up, I'm dropping dead.

A devoted daughter gives her visiting mother a roast chicken in a zip-up bag to take home to Golders Green. The mother gets on the train, and places the bag beside her. Dozing, she doesn't notice that a man sits down next to her and puts the chicken on the floor. Meanwhile, the mother unzips his trousers and puts her hand on his penis. She purrs: 'What a daughter I have – the neck of the chicken is still warm!'

—[*on the phone*] Hello, darling, it's Mummy. How are you?

—Oh, Mummy, I'm having a rough day. The kids are acting up, the washing machine's broken, the house is a mess and I haven't prepared dinner.

—Don't worry, dear, I'll be right over. I'll take the kids to the park, phone the washing machine repair man, clean the house and then I'll cook dinner for you and David.

—David? Who's David?

—Why, he's your husband… This is 020-600-87, isn't it?

—No, this is 020-600-86.

—Oh, I'm sorry, I must have dialled the wrong number.

—Does this mean you're not coming over?

A Jewish mother is standing at the edge of a stormy sea. 'Help, help!' she cries. 'What's the matter?' asks a passer-by. She explains, 'My son, the lawyer, is drowning!'

—What's the difference between a Rottweiler and a Jewish mother?

—Eventually the Rottweiler lets go.

Mine! Mine! Mine! Spoilt brats

Parents of young children should realise that few people, and maybe no one, will find their children as enchanting as they do.

Barbara Walters

If from infancy you treat children as gods they are liable in adulthood to act as devils.

P.D. James, The Children of Men

When you're the only pea in the pod, your parents are likely to get you confused with the Hope Diamond.

Russell Baker

True spoiling is nothing to do with what a child owns or what amount of attention he gets… It is not what he gets that is at issue. It is how and why he gets it.

Penelope Leach

Because I said so: Discipline

Parenting requires patience, endurance, forgiveness, understanding. And if the children aren't willing to do that, it's going to be tough.

Gene Perret

I'm told you spend the first two years desperate for your kids to talk, and then the rest of their lives telling them to shut up.

Catherine Zeta-Jones

I was a mouthy child and when my mother had enough she'd say, 'Come sit on my lap and we'll look up orphanages.'

Jackie Kashian

If you have never been hated by your child you have never been a parent.

Bette Davis

My mother was a vengeful person. She used to get up in the morning, and say, 'The Lord tells us to turn the other cheek, but there are only so many cheeks in a day.'

Jeanette Winterson

He's not the Messiah. He's a very naughty boy!

Brian's Mother, Monty Python's Life of Brian

—Did you hear what I said?
—Yes, I heard. If I cut my ears off I'd still be able to hear you through my nose!

Kate and Eugene, Brighton Beach Memoirs

I love it when mothers get so mad they can't remember your name: 'Come here, Roy, er, Rupert, er, Rutabaga… what is your name, boy? And don't lie to me, because you live here, and I'll find out who you are!'

Bill Cosby

This is as mad as my mother ever got: 'Ya'll quit! Don't make me stop this car!' 'Momma, you're not in the car. You're in a hammock with a jam-jar full of Scotch.'

Brett Butler

My mother never saw the irony in calling me a son-of-a-bitch.

Richard Jeni

—I will not fuck it up again, Mum.
—Bridget! Language!
—Sorry. I will not fuck it up again, _Mother_.

Bridget Jones and Mum, Bridget Jones, The Edge of Reason

If a mute kid swears, should his mother wash his hands with soap?

Steven Wright

At the mall I saw a kid on a leash. And I think if I ever have a kid, it's gonna be cordless.

Wendy Liebman

Your children vividly remember every unkind thing you ever did to them, plus a few you really didn't.

Mignon McLaughlin

My mother tried to kill me when I was a baby. She denied it. She said she thought the plastic bag would keep me fresh.

Bob Monkhouse

—Bart, you will not be getting a tattoo for Christmas.
—Yeah, if you want one, you'll have to pay for it out of your own allowance.

Marge and Homer Simpson

—You're doing that play, son, and that's all there is to it.
—Well, Dad said I didn't have to and Dad outranks you.
—Are you new here?

Roseanne and DJ, Roseanne

Son, your mother makes a very loud point.

Homer Simpson

Things a Mother Should Know: how to comfort a son without exactly saying Daddy was wrong.

Katharine Whitehorn, How to Survive Children

My kids can't agree on anything. We have a dog with five different names.

Phyllis Diller

I hate to stop my kids fighting. It's the only thing they do together.

Phyllis Diller

BEWARE OF THE CHILDREN

Sign on the House of Ma and Pa Kettle, The Egg and I

Children in a family are like flowers in a bouquet: there's always one determined to face in an opposite direction from the way the arranger desires.

Marcelene Cox

Why don't I just put them back in me and cook 'em until they're civilized?

Lynette Scavo, Desperate Housewives

We'd ask our mother what she wanted for her birthday and every year she'd say the same thing: 'What do I want for my birthday? I want my kids to get along. All I want is peace in this house.' Well, we saved a lot of money on gifts.

Judy Gold

Most children threaten at times to run away from home. This is the only thing that keeps some parents going.

Phyllis Diller

I told my mom I was gonna run away from home. She said, 'On your marks…'

Rodney Dangerfield

I grew up in a mobile home. When I was a kid, I ran away from home, and it followed me.

Jimmy Brogan

Every father says the same thing: 'Where's your mother?'

Bill Cosby

I'm the disciplinarian, Guy's the spoiler. He's the fun guy. I'm doctor's appointments and homework. He's good cop, I'm bad cop.

Madonna

My mother had a great deal of trouble with me, but I think she enjoyed it.

Mark Twain

How many kids does it take to turn off one light in the kitchen? Three. One to say, 'What light?' and two more to say, 'I didn't turn it on.'

Erma Bombeck

The quickest way for a parent to get a child's attention is to sit down and look comfortable.

Lane Olinghouse

If you want your children to listen, try talking softly – to someone else.

Ann Landers

Never allow your child to call you by your first name. He hasn't known you long enough.

Fran Lebowitz

That's the thing about independently minded children. You bring them up teaching them to question authority, and you forget that the very first authority they question is you.

Susan Sarandon

Always stick to your guns. I would recommend a Winchester and a Colt .45.

Phyllis Diller

I'm against corporal punishment. Mental torture is much more effective.

Lily Savage

With children, the carrot works better than the stick. Except, of course, when you are trying to get them to eat their carrots.

Marion Kaplinsky

Fine your kids a penny for every fight they have. I did this once and by night time their bicycles had second mortgages.

Phyllis Diller

Different threats work for different mothers. One I get results with is: 'Clean up your plate or you have to eat dessert.'

Phyllis Diller

No self-respecting mother would run out of intimidations on the eve of a major holiday.

Erma Bombeck

I know someone who knows someone who knows an elf. And if any of you children acts up, so help me I will call Santa and tell him you want socks for Christmas!

Lynette Scavo, Desperate Housewives

When you have kids, have you noticed how the grass always looks greener on the other side of the fence? That's because when you have kids, you don't have grass.

Phyllis Diller

Hot dogs always seem better out than at home; so do French fries; so do your children.

Mignon McLaughlin

Children are like farts – people quite like their own.

Graham Norton

Always be nice to your children because they are the ones who will choose your rest home.

Phyllis Diller

When my kids become wild and unruly, I use a nice safe playpen. When they're finished, I climb out.

Erma Bombeck

Mum's the word: Favourite expressions

Don't say 'she'. Who's 'she' – the cat's mother?

Close that door! You don't live in a barn.

It's rude to stare.

Just look at the state of you!

Get up those stairs this minute!

Don't forget to wash behind your ears. You have enough dirt in there to grow potatoes.

Did you flush?

Always put on clean underwear in the morning in case you get run over by a bus.

Somebody got out of bed on the wrong side today.

If you eat that now, you're going to spoil your dinner.

Eat up, there are millions of children starving in the world.

Your eyes are bigger than your mouth.

You're not going out like that!

Who's paying for all these clothes, anyway?

It's neither use nor ornament.

You're in and out like a dog at a fair.

Never a dull moment.

Just wait till you have children.

Don't sit so close to the TV or you'll go blind.

It'll never heal if you pick it.

Take care, you'll have someone's eye out with that.

Put that down! You don't know where it's been.

I've only got one pair of hands.

I'm at the end of my tether.

I don't care what 'everyone' is doing.

If everyone jumps in the lake, would you want me to let you do it, too?

As long as you live under my roof, you'll do as I say.

Why? Because I say so, and I'm your mother.

Don't use that tone of voice with me.

I'm not asking you; I'm telling you.

You're driving me up the wall.

It'll end in tears.

If you don't stop crying, I'll give you something to cry about.

Is this the thanks I get?

You treat this house like a hotel.

If I've told you once, I've told you a thousand times…

If I talked to my mother the way you talk to me…

Don't dawdle – quick's the word and sharp's the action!

If I have to come in there, somebody's going to be sorry!

I'm going to count to three, one…two…two and a half…

Never mind! I'll do it myself.

Anything for a quiet life.

Momma would say, 'Wait till your father gets home!' 'Momma, it's been eight years.'

Brett Butler

My mom always said, 'Keep your chin up!' That's how I ran into the door.

Daryl Hogue

'And tired' always followed 'sick': worst beating I ever got in my life, my mother said, 'Well I am just sick…' I said, '…and tired.' I don't remember anything after that.

Bill Cosby

My mother used to say, 'Haven't I been telling you for the past half hour, I'm coming in a minute?'

E. Jean Crossland

My mum used to say stuff like, 'You're about as much use as a one-legged man in an arse-kicking contest.'

Ricky Gervais

My mother would say, 'That's the last time I'm gonna tell you to take out the garbage.' Well, thank God.

George Wallace

Having kids around the house I realise the stupid things I say to them that my parents used to say.

Like, 'Stop making faces or you'll stay that way.' I remember looking at one of my uncles thinking, 'So that's what happened to him.'

Maria Menozzi

Sooner or later we all quote our mothers.

Bern Williams

Kiss it better: Health

The best medicine in the world is a mother's kiss.

Anon

A mother's arms are more comforting than anyone else's.

Diana, Princess of Wales

When I was young, if any of us kids got sick, my mother would bring out the chicken soup. Of course, that didn't work for broken bones. For broken bones she gave us boiled beef.

George Burns

Don't follow the adage, 'Feed a cold'. I did once and the way I cook it turned into pneumonia.

Phyllis Diller

I used to sleep-walk, but my mother cured me with psychology. Scattered thumb tacks on the floor.

B.J. Hunnicutt, M*A*S*H

A frantic mother called the doctor late one night. 'Please hurry,' she said, 'my little boy's swallowed a ballpoint pen.' 'I'll be there in 20 minutes,' said the doctor. 'What should I do until you get here?' the mother asked anxiously. 'Use a pencil.'

Anon

As every mother must face, there comes a time when you have to give way to modern medicine and a kiss from Mummy is no match for keyhole surgery.

Mrs Merton

Domestic goddess: Housework

Now, as always, the most automated appliance in
any household is the mother.

Beverly Jones

Mothers will clean up everything. Scientists
have proven that a mom's spit is the exact chemical
composition of Formula 409. Moms spit on a
Kleenex. You get rust off a bumper with that
thing.

Jeff Foxworthy

My mother is a clean freak. She vacuumed so much,
the guy downstairs went bald.

Steve Bridges

If I'm sitting on the toilet and looking at the
grouting on the tiles, that grouting really gets to me.
Mothers have a thing about grouting.

Sharon Osbourne

I have a horror of leaving this world and not having anyone in the entire family know how to replace a toilet tissue spindle.

Erma Bombeck

My mother wrapped the living room furniture in plastic. We practised safe-sitting in our household.

Adam Ferrara

I had the plastic-furniture-you-couldn't-sit-on house. It's like living in a museum – towels you could never touch, china that no one's ever gonna use. Everything in my mother's house is for a special occasion that hasn't happened yet. The Pope may show up…

Ray Romano

I wouldn't bring friends home because everything was covered in plastic; the sofas, the lamps, wall hangings, even the trinkets on the tables were still in their boxes… Whenever I'd come home, I always half-expected to find my father covered in the plastic, dust-free, dead and perfectly preserved.

Ruby Wax, How Do You Want Me?

My mother is so neurotic. She puts down toilet paper on the seat even at our relative's house – at the dinner table.

Wendy Liebman

Everybody wants to save the earth; nobody wants to help Mom do the dishes.

P.J. O'Rourke

If evolution really works, how come mothers still have only two hands?

Ed Dussault

—[*on the phone*] Mum, I just gave birth to triplets! You know, triplets are conceived only once in every three million times!
—Good heavens, darling, when did you ever have time to do the housework?

Anon

I hate housework. You make the beds, you wash the dishes, and six months later you have to start all over again.

Joan Rivers

Her refrigerator door has so many fingerprints on it the FBI uses it to train agents.

Bob Hope

If your house is really a mess and a stranger comes to the door greet him with, 'Who could have done this? We have no enemies.'

Phyllis Diller

You could say, 'I would have cleaned but I'm helping my son's paediatrician conduct an allergy test.'

Phyllis Diller

The day I get excited about cleaning my house is the day Sears comes out with a ride-on vacuum cleaner.

Roseanne

If the kids write their names in the dust on the furniture, don't let them put the year.

Phyllis Diller

—Mummy, where does dust come from?
—Cremated fairies.

Jil Evans

Cleaning your house while your kids are still growing is like shovelling the walk before it stops snowing.

Phyllis Diller

Even when freshly washed and relieved of all obvious confections, children tend to be sticky.

Fran Lebowitz

Don't worry about bugs on your plants unless you have artificial plants.

Phyllis Diller

My mother from time to time puts on her wedding dress. Not because she's sentimental. She just gets really far behind in her laundry.

Brian Kiley

Have you ever taken anything back out of the dirty-clothes basket because it had become, relatively, the cleaner thing?

Katharine Whitehorn

I'm 18 years behind in my ironing. There's no use doing it now, it doesn't fit anybody I know.

Phyllis Diller

—Oh, I hate folding sheets!
—That's your underwear!
—Well, whatever it is, it's a two-man job. Where's Bart?

Homer and Marge Simpson

To get a roasting dish clean, send something like baked apples in it to a neighbour. Neighbours always return pans spotless, and you won't have to use a blow torch on it like you usually do.

Phyllis Diller

Buy yourself a cup that says 'To the World's Best Mom'. People's attitude about your house softens a lot with this staring them in the face.

Phyllis Diller

I have two kids, and over the years I developed a really relaxed attitude about the whole child-rearing thing. I don't cry over spilt milk. Spilt vodka, that's another story.

Darryl Hodge

At the worst, a house unkept cannot be so distressing as a life unlived.

Rose Macaulay

Just like Mama used to make: Food & drink

In the childhood memories of every good cook, there's a large kitchen, a warm stove, a simmering pot and mom.

Barbara Costikyan

Italian and Jewish families in my neighbourhood were very similar. Especially the mothers. The mothers whose world revolved around food. Who believed any problem could be solved with food. The mother who could never accept that you were actually full.

Ray Romano

Mother cooked for nine. I was an only child, but she cooked for nine.

John Goodman

My mother is famous in our family for favouring a kill-by rather than a sell-by date.

Ruth Watson

Most turkeys taste better the day after; my mother's tasted better the day before.

Rita Rudner

We didn't call it the kitchen in our house. We called it the Burns Unit. 'It's a bit burned,' my mother would say apologetically at every meal.

Bill Bryson, The Life and Times of the Thunderbolt Kid

Nothing comes out of that oven that you couldn't successfully resurface a road with.

Ria Parkinson, Butterflies

—I may pop by later with some of my mother's drop scones.

—Good, we can build a rockery.

Nick Swainey and Victor Meldrew, One Foot in the Grave

When I was a kid my mother would make chopped liver… Who wants to eat liver? That's the organ that filters out all the crap you eat. I'd look at the liver on my plate and worry, that could have been an alcoholic cow.

Joel Warshaw

If I didn't cook the way I do, my husband would never have been able to buy enough for our five kids. They've yet to ask for seconds.

Phyllis Diller

For thirty years my mother served the family nothing but leftovers. The original meal has never been found.

Calvin Trillin

In a child's lunchbox, a mother's thoughts.

Japanese proverb

Kids will eat anything – snot, scabs, soil, ear wax, toenail clippings. But not sprouts.

Tony Burgess

In general my children refused to eat anything that hadn't danced on TV.

Erma Bombeck

I would rather die than let my kid eat instant soup.

Gwyneth Paltrow

Most vegetables are something God invented to let mothers get even with their children.

P.J. O'Rourke

A food is not necessarily essential just because your child hates it.

Katharine Whitehorn, How to Survive Children

The best way to prevent your children from eating fatty, greasy, disgusting, unhealthy food is: don't let them eat from your plate.

Bill Dodds

Little kids in supermarkets buy cereal the way men buy lingerie. They get stuff they have no interest in just to get the prize inside.

Jeff Foxworthy

My mom was a little weird. When I was little, she would make chocolate frosting, and let me lick the beaters. And then she'd turn them off.

Marty Cohen

A menopausal mother and an electric carving knife – not a good combination.

Jenny Eclair

When I was growing up, my mother refused to bake. She said, 'Why, you'll just eat it.'

Betsy Salkind

Ask your child what he wants for dinner only if he's buying.

Fran Lebowitz

I don't wanna say we eat out a lot, but I've noticed that lately when I call my kids for dinner they run to the car.

Julie Kidd

—What did the waiter ask the group of dining Jewish mothers?
—Is anything all right?

Anon

My mother complained about her order in a restaurant and tried to send it back. I had to stop her. 'Ma, you can't send back food after you've finished eating it!'

Roberta Rockwell

Beware of the man who loves his mother's macaroni and cheese more than he loves sex. Or you. Or anything.

Linda Stasi

When a man talks to you about his mother's cooking, pay no attention, for between the ages of 12 and 21, a boy can eat large quantities of anything and never feel it.

Sarah Tyson Rorer

Top ten Murphy's laws for mums

All babies are born between midnight and 5am.

Murphy's Law

One child is not enough, but two children are far too many.

O'Toole's Axiom

A show-off is any child who is more talented than yours.

Mom's Law

The lost sock reappears only after its match has been discarded.

Mrs Fergus's Observation

The bag that breaks is the one with the eggs.

Woodside's Grocery Principle

Ovens either overcook or undercook. Microwave ovens overcook and undercook at the same time.

Murphy's Law

A child will not spill on a dirty floor.

Skoff's Law

147

We can childproof our homes, but they still get in.

Davis's Dictum

A surprise monetary windfall will be accompanies by an unexpected expense of the same amount.

First Law of Money Dynamics

Just after you've made both ends meet, someone moves the ends.

Berkshire's Law of Household Budgeting

Do you think money grows on trees? Money matters

The easiest way for your children to learn about money is for you not to have any, and then it's only too clear the jug pours out only what it contains.

Katharine Whitehorn, How to Survive Children

I was born in very sorry circumstances. My mother was sorry and my father was sorry as well.

Norman Wisdom

We were poor. If I wasn't a boy, I wouldn't have had nothing to play with.

Redd Foxx

I had a happy childhood. We were poor, but we were shoplifters.

Lily Savage

My mom used to save money by shopping at the Army-Navy Surplus store. I felt ridiculous going to school dressed as a Japanese Admiral.

Blamo Risher

My mom thinks coupons are money, and gives them as gifts.

Jayne Warren

The last thing any of my kids ever did for money was lose their baby teeth.

Phyllis Diller

How can a child resist the tooth fairy?… When I was broke, I pulled out my brother's teeth. Naturally, it was too good to last.

A. Whitney Brown

My eight-year-old bought a bicycle with money he had saved by not smoking.

Phyllis Diller

The teenager lost a contact lens while playing basketball in his driveway. After a fruitless search, he told his mother the lens was nowhere to be found. Undaunted she went outside and in a few minutes returned with the lens in her hand. 'I really looked hard for that, Mom,' said the youth. 'How'd you manage to find it?' 'We weren't looking for the same thing,' she replied. 'You were looking for a small piece of plastic. I was looking for $150.'

Ohio Motorist *magazine*

Children are rarely in the position to lend one a truly interesting sum of money. There are, however, exceptions, and such children are an excellent addition to any party.

Fran Lebowitz

I don't have a bank account because I don't know my mother's maiden name.

Paula Poundstone

Life was a lot simpler when what we honoured was father and mother rather than all major credit cards.

Robert Orben

My mother said, 'No matter how hard you hug your money, it never hugs you back.'

H. Jackson Brown

Another good thing about being poor is that when you are 70 your children will not have you declared legally insane in order to gain control of your estate.

Woody Allen

If you want your child to turn out well, spend twice as much time with them, and half as much money.

Abigail Van Buren

Money isn't everything, but it sure keeps you in touch with your children.

John Paul Getty

I want my children to have all the things I couldn't afford. Then I want to move in with them.

Phyllis Diller

Don't make me stop this car! Travel

A suburban mother's role is to deliver children obstetrically once, and by car forever after.

Peter De Vries

Travelling with kids is terrible. This is the way we figure mileage – how many miles to a fight. We stopped for a hitchhiker once, he took one look and refused to get in.

Phyllis Diller

Things a Mother Should Know: how to drive a car safely with the children's hands over her eyes.

Katharine Whitehorn, How to Survive Children

Safety was not a big thing when I was growing up. A seatbelt was something that got in the way. I'd be like, 'Ma, the seat belt is digging into my back.' 'Stuff it down into the seat. And roll those windows up, you're letting the cigarette smoke out!'

Margaret Smith

My mom taught me to drive. I can't drive worth a damn, but I can change all my clothes at a stoplight.

Craig Shoemaker

Never lend your car to anyone to whom you have given birth.

Erma Bombeck

Cyber mum: Mums & technology

VCRs were like Kryptonite to my mother... She was actually afraid of it. Whenever she was yelling at me for something, I'd just pick it up and scare her out of the room. 'Back it up, Ma... look what I got!'

Ray Romano

My mother emails me and then calls me to tell me she sent an email… 'Did it get through?' Yes, about 40 times. Stop pressing 'send'. I had to report my mother for spam.

Maria Menozzi

My dear mother is determined to master the new technology: she typed an email to me on the computer, printed it out, popped it in an envelope and posted it to me.

John O'Farrell

I get so many really dull mouse mats in celebrity goodie bags that I give them to my mother. She doesn't know what they are, of course. She sets the table with them… There are 24 of you 'round for lunch and you've all got mouse mats.

Jenny Eclair

—Mother, are you still on the computer?
—Yes, dear. Sometimes you get into a porn loop and just can't get out.

Edina Monsoon and Mum, Absolutely Fabulous

Mother is far too clever to understand anything she does not like.

Arnold Bennett

At my mother's knee: Education

Education commences at the mother's knee, and every word spoken within the hearing of little children tends towards the formation of character.

Hosea Ballou

At My Mother's Knee…And Other Low Joints
Paul O'Grady, title of autobiography

All parents think their kids are the smartest kids ever born. My mom thought my daughter was a genius because she would lie on the floor and talk to the ceiling fan. I said, 'Mom, Uncle Harold does that, and you call him an alcoholic.'

Jeff Foxworthy

All mothers think their children are oaks, but the world never lacks for cabbages.

Robertson Davies

If there were no schools to take children away from home part of the time, the insane asylums would be filled with mothers.

E. W. Howe

Try to control your emotions when your children leave the house the first day of school. Once I turned a cartwheel and broke my ankle.

Phyllis Diller

The first time you leave your child at school you're faced with a tough decision – down the pub or back to bed?

Jo Brand

My dear, dear Mother, If you don't let me come home, I die – I am all over ink, and my fine clothes have been spoilt – I have been tost in a blanket, and seen a ghost. I remain, my dear, dear mother, Your most dutiful and most unhappy son, Freddy.

P.S. Remember me to my father.

Frederick Reynolds, aged 7, letter to his mother after two days at Westminster School, London, c.1775

Mum was having a tough time getting her son ready for school. 'I'm not going!' he screamed. 'The teachers all make fun of me and the kids all hate me. I'm just not going anymore.' 'I'll give you two reasons why you will go, son,' said the mother. 'First, you are 49, and second, you're the headmaster.'

Anon

Mom, if I was bleeding out of my ears, you'd make me go to school.

Jeanie Bueller, Ferris Bueller's Day Off

—But I thought you liked school.

—I like peanut butter but I don't want it every day.

Annie and Ruthie Camden, 7th Heaven

When my kid came home I asked him what he did all day, and he said the teacher asked him to cut some things out. I asked him what they were and he said, 'Smoking and swearing.'

Phyllis Diller

If Everybody Else's Mother turned up at the PTA meeting and identified herself, she would be lynched.

Erma Bombeck

As we read the school report on our children, we realise a sense of relief that can rise to delight that – thank heaven – nobody is reporting in this fashion on us.

J.B. Priestley

Thank God for falling standards.

Relieved mother, on seeing her son's excellent A-level results, 2004

The best academy: a mother's knee.

James Russell Lowell

All I ever learned at my mother's knee was what a
bony knee looked like.

Phyllis Diller

Growing pains

You know your kids are growing up when they start
asking questions to which there are answers.

John J. Plomp

The way we know the kids are growing up: the bite
marks are higher.

Phyllis Diller

Children are angels whose wings decrease as their
legs increase

French proverb

I've noticed that the one thing about parents is that
no matter what stage your child is in, the parents
who have older children always tell you the next
stage is worse.

Dave Barry

My eleven-year-old daughter mopes around the house all day waiting for her breasts to grow.

Bill Cosby

It kills you to see them grow up. But I guess it would kill you quicker if they didn't.

Barbara Kingsolver

Where do babies come from? Sex education

There's a time when you have to explain to your children why they're born, and it's a marvellous thing if you know the reason by then.

Hazel Scott

—Where do babies come from? I heard a hideous story about it once in the schoolyard.
—Oh. Well, it's true, I'm afraid.

Lisa and Marge Simpson

I blame my mother for my poor sex life. All she told me about sex was that the man goes on top and the woman underneath. For three years my husband and I slept in bunk beds.

Joan Rivers

Jenni Murray says mothers are tormented when their sons discover sex. We'd be much more tormented if they didn't.

Lynda Lee-Potter

I didn't know how babies were made until I was pregnant with my fourth child five years later.

Loretta Lynn, country singer, married aged 13

My mom said, 'Sex is a dirty and disgusting thing you save for someone you love.'

Carol Henry

My mother is sixty, and her whole life she only slept with one guy. She won't tell me who.

Wendy Liebman

I'm a virgin and I brought up all my children to be the same.

Shirley Bassey

My mother used to say, Delia, if S-E-X ever rears its ugly head, close your eyes before you see the rest of it.

Delia, Bedroom Farce *by Alan Ayckbourn*

While we were washing dishes, suddenly out of the blue, my mother said: 'If a man ever asks you to do something funny to him, tell him to go to hell, you hear?…That's why the French can't win a war without our help. It saps their strength. They spend all their time doing something funny to each other.'

Florence King, American author, on oral sex

—Do you have sexual relations, Mummy?
—Well, yes, dear, I do.
—Can we go and visit them some time?

Young daughter and mother

I was watching television one evening with my wife and mother, aged 90, when a rather risqué scene appeared. My wife, a little embarrassed, wanted to change channels but my mother stopped her by saying, 'Don't do that. We might learn something!'

George Jamieson

Watching sex on telly with Mum and Dad: that's embarrassing. I didn't even know they knew how to use the camcorder.

Jimmy Carr

Things Children Should Know – But Don't: that Mummy and Daddy don't actually do all that *just* to make a baby.

Katharine Whitehorn, How to Survive Children

My husband explained the facts of life to the kids one day and when it was all over I asked one of the boys what he wants to be when he grows up. He said: 'Either a bird or a bee.'

Phyllis Diller

My biology teacher friend described the human sex act to a class of pupils aged 15 to 16. A voice called out: 'My mum and dad still do it and they're 50.' The entire class let out a 'Yuck'. My friend, 50, could only smile.

Pam Cheshire

People want to take sex education out of the schools. They believe sex education causes promiscuity. Hey, I took Algebra. I never do math.

Elayne Boosler

Telling a teenager the facts of life is like giving a fish a bath.

Arnold Glasgow

After they stop asking where they came from, they start telling you where to go.

Phyllis Diller

There are only two things a Jewish Mother needs to know about sex and marriage: 1) Who is having sex? 2) Why aren't they married?

Dan Greenburg

My mother used to give all my school friends, when they got married, a Kenwood Chef and a copy of the 'Kama Sutra'. She said it was all they needed in marriage.

Clarissa Dickson Wright

The best sex education for kids is when Daddy pats Mommy on the [rear] when he comes home from work.

William H. Masters

Like, whatever: Teenagers

It's amazing. One day you look at your phone bill and realise they're teenagers.

Milton Berle

Childhood is a time of rapid changes. Between the ages of 12 and 17, a parent can age thirty years.

Sam Levenson

No one knows his true character until he has run out of gas, purchased something on the instalment plan and raised an adolescent.

Marcelene Cox

Adolescence is that period in a kid's life when his or her parents become more difficult.

Ryan O'Neal

Oh, to be half as wonderful as my child thought I was when he was small, and only half as stupid as my teenager now thinks I am.

Rebecca Richards

Living with a teenage daughter is like living with the Taliban. Mothers are not allowed to dance, sing, flirt, laugh loudly or wear short skirts.

Kathy Lette

It's great how my menopause coincides with my kid's puberty. This way we can all be miserable.

Mum's the Word

Teenagers are hormones with feet.

Marsha Doble

One of our kids lay sprawled out in a living room chair so continuously that when he got sick we didn't know whether to call a doctor or an upholsterer.

Phyllis Diller

My teenage son is half-man, half-mattress.

Val Valentine

My friends complain that their teenagers sleep all day. Not me. Can you imagine if they were awake all day? Teenagers, like espresso, are meant to be taken in small doses.

Buzz Nutley

The invention of the teenager was a mistake. Once you identify a period in life in which people get to stay out late but don't have to pay taxes – naturally, nobody wants to live any other way.

Judith Martin

On my sixteenth birthday my parents tried to
surprise me with a car – but they missed.

Tom Cotter

The best way to keep children home is to make the
home atmosphere pleasant – and let the air out of
their tyres.

Dorothy Parker

My teenage son, Harry, was off out to a party. 'Have
a great time!' I called after him. 'Mum, stop telling
me what to do!' the young rebel called back.

Sue Blake

Imagination is something that sits up with Dad and
Mom the first time their teenager stays out late.

Lane Olinghouse

No need to worry about your teenagers when they're
not at home. A national survey revealed that they all
go to the same place – 'out' – and they all do the
same thing there – 'nothing'.

Bruce Lansky

There's nothing wrong with teenagers that reasoning with them won't aggravate.

Jean Kerr

There are few things more satisfying than seeing your children have teenagers of their own.

Doug Larson

You're not going out like that! Mums & fashion

A child develops individuality long before he develops taste. I have seen my kids straggle into the kitchen in the morning with outfits that need only one accessory: an empty gin bottle.

Erma Bombeck

Whenever my mother sees me she says, 'Jenny, Jenny, why aren't you wearing a petticoat?' 'Mother, it's because I've got jeans on.'

Jenny Eclair

My mother buys me those big granny panties, three in a pack. You can use them for a car cover.

Monique Marvez

I knew I looked awful because my mother phoned and said I looked lovely.

Jo Brand, after a 'Trinny and Susannah' TV makeover

Daphne, dear, I finally figured out what's wrong with your outfit: it's made for a smaller woman.

Gertrude Moon, Frasier

All women dress like their mothers, that is their tragedy. No man ever does. That is his.

Alan Bennett

I'm coming out: Sexuality

It's better to be black than gay because when you're black you don't have to tell your mother.

Charles Pierce

When asked, 'Shall I tell my mother I'm gay?' I reply, 'Never tell your mother anything.'

Quentin Crisp

When I came out, my mother said, 'Oh, darling! Why can't you just be like a normal man: get married to a woman, and keep a boy in Soho?' I declined that offer.

Rabbi Roderick Young

When I came out, my mom said, 'I'd love you even if you were a murderer.'

Marc Cherry

I came out at Thanksgiving. I said, 'Mom, would you please pass the gravy to a homosexual?' And she passed it to my father.

Bob Smith

I'm just a man who's very good to his mother.

John 'I'm Free' Inman

I wanted her to grow up, get married, have a child, get divorced and live happily ever after.

Cher, on her daughter, Chastity Bono

Every year on Christmas day I like to tell my mother that I'm a lesbian, even though I'm not. It just gets everything going.

Jenny Eclair

Don't get me wrong. I support whatever your sexual preference is as long as you're committed. I myself can't believe I will eventually have to marry someone the same sex as my mother.

Garry Shandling

Ma, he's making eyes at me: Dating

He that would the daughter win must with the mother first begin.

17th-century English proverb

She was no different from all other mothers…in that while she wanted me, in a general way, to be married, she didn't want me, in a specific way, to have a wife.

Howard Jacobson, Peeping Tom

He's very careful who he brings home. He doesn't bring any of his lap dancers on a pole here.

Simon Cowell's mother

With our boys, when they came back with girlfriends, I'd be on my high horse about respecting girls and treating them properly while Tony would be: 'Go for it, young man.' But with Kathryn [our daughter] every boy who crosses the threshold is threatened with execution. I have said to him: 'This is ridiculous, Tony!'

Cherie Blair

Psychiatrists say girls tend to marry men like their fathers. That is probably the reason mothers cry at weddings.

Anon

At the age of 20, Bob Monkhouse was disowned by his parents after marrying his first wife, Elizabeth. His mother turned up at the wedding in mourning black.

BBC news website

Recently, my husband started worrying about the cost of our daughter's wedding, so he bought an aluminium ladder that he said *anybody* could lift.

Phyllis Diller

My mum promised me I could have the wedding I want, as soon as I have a daughter who gets engaged.

Daphne Moon, Frasier

I went out with one girl who said, 'Don't treat me like a date, treat me like you would your mom.' So I didn't call her for six months.

Zorba Jevon

My mother is terrified that I'll get married before I sow my wild oats.

Molly Ringwald

My mom always said, 'Men are like linoleum floors. You lay them right, and you can walk on them for thirty years.'

Brett Butler

My mom said the only reason men are alive is for lawn care and vehicle maintenance.

Tim Allen

My mother said it was simple to keep a man: you must be a maid in the living room, a cook in the kitchen and a whore in the bedroom. I said I'd hire the other two and take care of the bedroom bit.

Jerry Hall

My mother always said, 'Don't marry for money. Divorce for money.'

Wendy Liebman

My son is gay, but thank God he's dating a very nice Jewish doctor.

Jewish mother

I was dating a transvestite, and my mother said,
'Marry him. You'll double your wardrobe.'

Joan Rivers

Every man of any age group who has ever gone out
with someone who has a stunning mother will have
had fantasies about her. Older women have this
inner self-confidence and are confident with their
bodies. I find that sexy in a woman.

Nicholas Bailey

You look too young to be her mother – oh, apart
from your neck.

Eric Gartside to Shelley Unwin's mum, Coronation Street

My mother was desperate to get me married. She
used to say, 'Sure, he's a murderer. But he's a *single*
murderer.'

Joan Rivers

Romance is dead. So is my mother. Man, 42,
inherited wealth. Box no 7652.

Personal Ad, London Review of Books

Letting go: The empty nest

A mother is not a person to lean on but a person to make leaning unnecessary.

Dorothy Canfield Fisher

I took a very practical view of raising children, I put a sign in each of their rooms: checkout time is 18 years.

Erma Bombeck

When I went to college, my parents threw a going away party for me, according to the letter.

Emo Philips

There isn't a child who hasn't gone out into the brave new world who eventually doesn't return to the old homestead carrying a bundle of dirty clothes.

Art Buchwald

Human beings are the only creatures that allow their children to come back home.

Bill Cosby

The true nightmare of the empty nest is that the kids were the only people in the house who knew how to use the remote control.

Nora Ephron

Do you miss me? Kids flying solo

Of course, now that I live 2,500 miles away, I miss Mom. I miss the worrying, the meals, the Vicks VapoRub.

Ray Romano

Things I won't miss about not living with me mum any more: I won't miss her shaving her legs with my Mach 3, but I will miss her being able to turn over a cauliflower cheese grill with the palm of her hand.

Peter Kay

I'm enjoying adulthood for a lot of reasons. Reason number one: as an adult, if I want a cookie, I have a cookie. I can have three cookies or four cookies, or eleven cookies. And then I call my mother to tell her: 'Hello, Mom? I just ruined my appetite.'

Jerry Seinfeld

I do not like broccoli. And I haven't liked it since I was a little kid and my mother made me eat it. I'm President of the United States, and I'm not going to eat any more broccoli.

George Bush Sr.

Dial M for Mama

Certain things in our universe are fixed and absolute. The sun always rises in the east. Parking meters are always set to give an edge to the meter warden. And sons never phone.

Brian Devlin, The Devlin Connection

My mother phones daily to ask, 'Did you just try to reach me?' When I reply, 'No,' she adds, 'So if you're not too busy, call while I'm still alive,' and hangs up.

Erma Bombeck

An answering machine is the stupidest gift to give your parents. No one ever calls them except for their kids.

Judy Gold

A Jewish mother's answering machine:
If you want chicken soup, press 1.
If you want matzoh balls with the soup, press 2.
If you want stuffed cabbage, press 3.
If you want a slice of sponge cake, press 4.
If you want to know how I'm feeling, you've dialled the wrong number since nobody ever asks me how I'm feeling.

Anon

Instead of saying hello, my mother gets on the phone and says, 'Guess who died?'

Dom Irrera

I got on the phone, my mom said, 'Hi! Is everything wrong?'

Richard Lewis

I call my daughter every single day. And she always says the same thing: 'How the hell did you get this number?'

Joan Rivers

[_answering the phone_] Bridget Jones, wanton sex goddess, with a very bad man between her thighs… Mum… Hi.

Bridget Jones, Bridget Jones's Diary

Keeping in touch

My mom wanted to know why I never get home for the holidays. I said, 'Because I can't get Delta Airlines to wait in the yard while I run in.'

Margaret Smith

Until I got married, when I used to go out, my mother said goodbye to me as though I was emigrating.

Thora Hird

I love my parents and they're wonderful people, but they were strict, and I still look for ways to get even. When I got my own apartment for the first time and they came to stay with me for the weekend, I made them stay in separate bedrooms.

Elayne Boosler

Nothing looks as lonely as your mom before she sees you coming up the platform.

Pam Brown

I've bought a flat on the 28th floor but my mum won't get in a lift, so she won't come to see me.

Steve Jones, TV presenter

Saw my mom today. It was all right, she didn't see me.

Margaret Smith

I get along great with my parents. I still talk to them at least once a week. It's the least I can do – I still live in their house.

David Corrado

Instant availability without continuous presence is probably the best role a mother can play.

Lotte Bailyn

The umbilical cord stretches like a nine-hundred-and-some-mile leash.

Peter De Vries

No matter how old a mother is, she watches her middle-aged children for signs of improvement.

Florida Scott-Maxwell

The relationship between mothers and children never changes and that's because no matter how rich or powerful you are your mother still remembers when you were three and put Spaghetti-Os up your nose.

Dennis Miller

Parenting is like your Aunt Edna's ass. It goes on for ever and it's just as frightening.

Frank Buckman, Parenthood

Top ten maternal sayings

The hand that rocks the cradle is the hand that rules the world.

William Ross Wallace

A child without a mother is like a door without a knob.

Jewish

Little children, little joys; big children, big worries.

Jewish

A child without a mother is like a curry without onions.

Telegu

A mother's children are like ideas; none are as wonderful as her own.

Chinese

Every beetle is a gazelle in the eyes of its mother.

Moorish

One mother can achieve more than a hundred teachers.

Jewish

A mother understands what a child does not say.

Jewish

The warmest bed of all is Mother's.

Jewish

The hand that rules the cradle rocks the world.

Peter De Vries

Like mother, like daughter: Mothers & daughters

As a rule there is only one person an English girl hates more than she hates her eldest sister; and that's her mother.

George Bernard Shaw

My daughter told me she thinks I'm a son of a bitch. She also thinks I'm a funny son of a bitch. She loves me but she doesn't like me. She's afraid of me, she's intimidated by me. She respects me, but she doesn't want to become like me. We have a perfectly normal mother–daughter relationship.

Hannah Warren, California Suite

My mother won't admit it, but I've always been a disappointment to her. Deep down inside, she'll never forgive herself for giving birth to a daughter who refuses to launder aluminium foil and use it over again.

Erma Bombeck

When my mother makes out her income tax return every year, under 'occupation' she writes in: 'Eroding my daughter's self-esteem.'

Robin Roberts

My mother and I could always look out the same window without ever seeing the same thing.

Gloria Swanson

I'm very close to my daughter, but I'm careful not to ask personal questions, like, 'Hello?'

Joan Rivers

There are three books my daughter felt were the most important influences in her life: the Bible, her mother's cook book, and her father's cheque book.

Joyce Mattingly

There are many things I will never forgive my mother for, but heading the list is the fact that she did the Double-Crostic in ink.

Nora Ephron

If you're looking for a way to piss your mother off, here's what I suggest – and I actually did this: next time you're with your mother, stop in front of a local strip joint. Park the car and say, 'I'll be right back, I just have to run in and pick up my cheque.'

Judy Gold

I have reached the age when a woman begins to perceive that she is growing into the person she least plans to resemble: her mother.

Anita Brookner, Incidents in the Rue Laugier

Of all the haunting moments of motherhood, few rank with hearing your own words come out of your daughter's mouth.

Victoria Secunda

Oh, my son's my son till he gets him a wife, but my daughter's my daughter all her life.

Dinah Mulock Craik

Mummy's boy: Mothers & sons

What's harder to raise, boys or girls? Girls. Boys are easy. Give 'em a book of matches, and they're happy.

Etta May

My son doesn't smoke or drink or swear or stay out late. I just hope he'll still be as good when he leaves kindergarten.

Jane Anderson

Pamela Anderson has two gorgeous sons. They're actually the only two guys that have ever come *out* of Pam.

Sarah Silverman

A boy's best friend is his mother.

Norman Bates, Psycho

I'm very loyal in a relationship. When I go out with my mom, I don't look at other moms. I don't go, 'Oooh, I wonder what her macaroni and cheese tastes like.'

Garry Shandling

Few misfortunes can befall a boy which bring worse consequences than to have a really affectionate mother.

W. Somerset Maugham

My mother was like a sister to me, only we didn't have sex quite so often.

Emo Philips

We've begun to raise daughters more like sons… but few have the courage to raise our sons more like our daughters.

Gloria Steinem

The only time a woman really succeeds in changing a man is when he is a baby.

Natalie Wood

Frankly, I'm two breasts away from being exactly like my mother. Which is not good.

Richard Lewis

All women become like their mothers. That is their tragedy. No man does. That's his.

Oscar Wilde

Life lessons for Mum

The moment you have children yourself, you forgive your parents everything.

Susan Hill

Parents can be so busy with the physical rearing of children that they miss the glory of parenthood, just as the grandeur of the trees is lost when raking leaves.

Marcelene Cox

Having a child is nothing like it is on the Persil adverts. Nothing so good is ever that anodyne.

Louise Wener

Children reinvent your world for you.

Susan Sarandon

Whenever I held my newborn baby in my arms, I used to think that what I said and did to him could have an influence not only on him but on all whom he met, not only for a day or a month or a year, but for all eternity – a very challenging and exciting thought for a mother.

Rose Kennedy, mother of President John F. Kennedy

If there were no other reasons (though we know there are as many as stars), this alone would be the value of children: the way they remind you of the comfort of simplicity. Their compelling common sense. Their accessibility and their honesty. Their lack of pretence.

Elizabeth Berg

I guess what I've really discovered is the humanising effect of children in my life – stretching me, humbling me. Maybe my thighs aren't as thin as they used to be. Maybe my getaways aren't as glamorous. Still I like the woman that motherhood has helped me to become.

Susan Lapinski

Your mother should know: Life lessons from Mum

Mother always said that honesty was the best policy, and money isn't everything. She was wrong about other things too.

Gerald Barzan

Mother's words of wisdom: 'Answer me! Don't talk with your mouth full!'

Erma Bombeck

Has anyone ever put an eye out running around with a sharp stick in their hand? My mother warned me about that every day of my childhood.

Lewis Grizzard

When I was a boy, my mother used to say to me, 'Never point your finger at anyone because when you do, three fingers are pointing back at you.'

Dr John Sentamu, Archbishop of York

My mother always told me never to accept candy from strange men. Get real estate instead.

Eva Gabor

My mum told me the best time to ask my dad for anything was during sex. Not the best advice I've ever been given. I burst in through the bedroom door saying, 'Can I have a new bike?' He was very upset. His secretary was surprisingly nice about it. I got the bike.

Jimmy Carr

My mother said, 'You won't amount to anything because you procrastinate.' I said, 'Just wait.'

Judy Tenuta

My mother thinks everything can be fixed with crafting and prayer: 'Let God and glue into your life.'

Monique Marvez

Never look at your feet – my mother taught me that.

Queen Elizabeth, the Queen Mother

A glass of wine with lunch? Is that wise? You know you have to reign all afternoon.

The Queen Mother, to Queen Elizabeth II

My momma always said life was like a box of chocolates – you never know what you're gonna get.

Forrest Gump

My mother said you should always buy a good pair of shoes and a good bed, because if you're not in one, you're in the other.

Gloria Hunniford

My mother gave me this advice: trust your husband, adore your husband and get as much as you can in your own name.

Joan Rivers

You know you can put up a front in the real world, but your mom sees through that faster than Superman sees through Lois Lane's pantsuits.

Dennis Miller

You can fool all of the people some of the time, and some of the people all of the time, but you can't fool Mom.

Captain Penny's Law

—It's at times like this I wish I'd listened to my mother.

—Why, what did she say?

—I don't know, I never listened.

Arthur and Ford, The Hitchhiker's Guide to the Galaxy

If it's not one thing, it's your Mother: Therapy

My family is so dysfunctional that when I looked up the word 'dysfunctional' in the dictionary there was a picture of my mother.

Paulara Hawkins

I told my mother that I was thinking about seeing a therapist. She thought that was a good idea because she heard they make a lot of money.

Darlene Hunt

I've been in therapy once a week for sixteen years. My friend thought that was rather extensive, so I brought her home to meet my family. Now she goes twice a week.

Cathy Ladman

A Jewish mother takes her teenage son to see a psychiatrist. At the end of the session the psychiatrist calls her into his office and says, 'Mrs Goldstein, your son has an Oedipus complex.' 'Oedipus Shmedipus,' she replies, 'as long as he loves his mother.'

Anon

You think Oedipus had a problem? Adam was Eve's mother.

Graffiti

He wrote me sad Mother's Day stories. He'd always kill me in the stories and tell me how bad he felt about it. It was enough to bring a tear to a mother's eye.

Connie Zastoupil, mother of Quentin Tarantino,
director of Pulp Fiction

—My mother made me a homosexual!
—If I give her the wool will she make me one, too?

Graffiti

Therapy is like a really easy game show where the answer to every question is, 'My mother.'

Robin Greenspan

In our society…mothers go on getting blamed until they're 80, but shouldn't take it personally.

Katharine Whitehorn

A child's incessant weeping, at first attributed by her worried custodians to an incest-complex, a mother-fixation and a malfunctioning gland, was eventually traced (to the mother's surprise) to wearing shoes two sizes too small.

Peter Vansittart

Most men are secretly still mad at their mothers for throwing out their comic books, which would be very valuable now.

Rita Rudner

Nowadays, parents take a 'problem' child to a psychiatrist to talk through difficulties. Grandad used the do-it-yourself method and took the kid fishing.

Eva Shaw

Never marry a man who hates his mother, because he'll end up hating you.

Jill Bennett

I'm as good a mother as the next repressed, obsessive-compulsive paranoiac.

Anne Lamott

Insanity is hereditary; you get it from your children.

Sam Levenson

My mother said I drove her crazy. I did not drive her crazy. I flew her there. It was faster.

Robin Tyler

In raising my children, I have lost my mind but found my soul.

Lisa T. Shepherd

Mama mia! Mum's influence

All that I am or ever hope to be, I owe to my angel mother.

Abraham Lincoln

Son, take this guitar – you're *not* going to get a rifle. Take it and play.

Gladys Love Smith, mother of Elvis Presley

What the mother sings to the cradle goes all the way down to the coffin.

Henry Ward Beecher

The future destiny of the child is always the work of the mother.

Napoleon Bonaparte

Children are likely to live up to what you believe of them.

Claudia 'Lady Bird' Johnson

The doctors told me that I would never walk, but my mother told me I would, so I believed my mother.

Wilma Rudolph, polio-sufferer who went on to become a triple Olympic gold medallist in track and field

In my interest she left no wire unpulled, no stone unturned, no cutlet uncooked.

Winston Churchill

A mother…is forever surprised and even faintly wronged that her sons and daughters are just people, for many mothers hope and half expect that their newborn child will make the world better, will somehow be a redeemer.

Florida Scott-Maxwell

My mother said to me, 'If you become a soldier, you'll be a general; if you become a monk, you'll end up as the Pope.' Instead, I became a painter, and wound up as Picasso.

Pablo Picasso

Mother – WE won the Nobel Prize.

Telegram sent by Albert Einstein on winning the Nobel Prize for Physics, 1921

My mother was watching on television and she doesn't want me to hurt anyone.

George Foreman, US 1968 Olympic gold medallist in boxing, on why he didn't knock out his Soviet opponent

My parents' dream was for me to have everything they didn't. And thanks to ozone holes, fear of AIDS and no health insurance, their dream has come true.

Brad Slaight

Mother's pride and joy

—Are you proud of your son?
—Which one?

Interviewer and Mrs Eisenhower, mother of
President Dwight D. Eisenhower

When my mother saw my name come up on screen she wept, and I said, 'Mum, that's really the best part, now it's just going to be sex and violence for the next ninety minutes.'

Clive Barker, actor, star of Hellraiser

This is a moment that I deeply wish my parents could have lived to share. My father would have enjoyed what you have so generously said of me – and my mother would have believed it.

President Lyndon B. Johnson, giving a commencement address at Baylor University

There are two kinds of mothers: those who place a child's bouquet in a milk bottle on top of the refrigerator, and those who enthrone it on the piano.

Marcelene Cox

A mother is never cocky nor proud, because she knows the school principal may call at any minute to report that her child has just driven a motorcycle through the gymnasium.

Mary Kay Blakely

Golden oldies

When I was six years old I asked my late (and she made late an art) mother on her approaching birthday, in order to get her card correct, 'Are you going to be 36 or 63?'

Viscount Simon

—How old are you, Mummy?
—As old as my tongue and a little bit older than my teeth.

Anon

Children are a great comfort in your old age – and they help you reach it faster, too.

Lionel Kauffman

My mother is no spring chicken, although she has got as many chemicals in her as one.

Dame Edna Everage

My mother is going to have to stop lying about her age because pretty soon I'm going to be older than she is.

Tripp Evans

Recently I persuaded my mother to purchase a walking stick. For too long she has put off this moment, but now gripping it firmly in her right hand she takes enormous pleasure in beating the earwigs out of my dahlias, no matter that the blooms fly off as well.

Eleanor Baxter

My mother was 88 years old. She never used glasses. Drank right out of the bottle.

Henny Youngman

My father is now 76, my mother 68. Two years ago she finally gave herself a present she had been wanting for 45 years: a divorce.

Phillip Lopate

My 92-year-old mother says: 'The paint and plaster may be peeling and cracking on the outside but that doesn't matter if the rooms inside are warm and cosy.'

Wilbur Smith

My mother's suffering from advanced Old-Timer's disease so we've put her in a maximum security Twilight Home For the Bewildered called Dunraven.

Dame Edna Everage

I took the liberty of checking out a few convalescent homes…'Golden Acres: We Care, so You Don't Have to'.

Niles Crane, Frasier

I'm pretty good at spotting the warning signs of death: your children start visiting you during the week.

Sophia Petrillo, The Golden Girls

My 84-year-old mother still plays competition bowls. During a match in the recent hot spell she fainted. After coming round and drinking a glass of water she insisted on continuing the game – which she won. Father, 86, said: 'You could have died.' 'And what a wonderful way to go,' was her reply.

Christina Page

Losing Mum

—Mother? Mother? Where are you?
—Your mother can't be with you anymore.

Bambi and the Great Prince of the Forest, Bambi

After Patricia rang and told me my mother had died, I watched the television news. I found it amazing that they did not announce her death. The world had altered and I thought that the world would be interested. But it was not. I discovered that as Icarus fell out of the sky, as in the Auden poem, 'The Musée des Beaux Arts', the ploughman went on ploughing and the dog went on about its doggy business.

Kate Llewellyn, The Dressmaker's Daughter

I have no idea if it's possible to do it without her or if I want to.

Maureen Lipman, on the death of her mother, Zelma

Fields and meadows can never be the same to you as a human being; they can't laugh with you when you're happy; nor comfort you when you're sad. Nothing on earth can make up for the loss of one who has loved you.

Selma Lagerlöf

Sorrow makes us all children again – destroys all differences of intellect. The wisest know nothing.

Ralph Waldo Emerson

The death of a mother is the first sorrow wept without her.

Anon

That lovely voice; how I should weep for joy I if I could hear it now!

Colette

I went into the kitchen and got halfway to the phone before I realised that I couldn't call her... A lot of people who lost a mother...will tell you that they find themselves almost talking out loud. I do that a lot.

Bill Clinton

Mom died in 1998. My son was born in 1999. When something great happens, I long to talk to her.

Mallory Lewis

My mother drove me crazy my entire life... and I will miss her for the rest of my own.

Shelley Berkley

I'd like to believe in heaven, not least because I'd like to meet my mum and dad again. I'd like to know whether the Welsh dresser was meant to go to me or my brother, really.

John Peel

When I approach the pearly gates, I'd like to hear a champagne cork popping, an orchestra tuning up, and the sound of my mother laughing.

Patricia Routledge

A mother's love for the child of her body differs essentially from all other affections, and burns with so steady and clear a flame that it appears like the one unchangeable thing in this earthly mutable life, so that when she is no longer present it is still a light to our steps and a consolation.

W.H. Hudson

A mother holds her children's hands for a while, their hearts forever.

Anon

Mother love

You never realise how much your mother loves you till you explore the attic – and find every letter you ever sent her, every finger painting, clay pot, bead necklace, Easter chicken, cardboard Santa Claus, paper lace Mother's Day card, and school reports since day one.

Pam Brown

We never know the love of our parents for us till we have become parents.

Henry Ward Beecher

When she'd had her first baby she had realised with astonishment that the perfect couple consisted of a mother and child and not, as she had always supposed, a man and a woman.

Alice Thomas Ellis, The Other Side of the Fire

You don't have to deserve your mother's love. You have to deserve your father's. He's more particular.

Robert Frost

Mother love is the cream of love.

Greek proverb

Priceless like a mother's love, or the good kind of priceless?

Bart Simpson

A man loves his sweetheart the most, his wife the best, but his mother the longest.

Irish proverb

You don't really understand human nature unless you know why a child on a merry-go-round will wave at his parents every time around – and why his parents will always wave back.

William D. Tammeus

I love my kids with a primal passion, but am occasionally tempted to put them back into the condom vending machine for a refund.

Kathy Lette

There's no way to repay a mother's love, or lack of it.

Mignon McLaughlin

—Mum, did you ever love us?
—I don't think so. I don't think I knew what love was till I bred my first Afghan.

Margaret and Stella, Pat and Margaret

Men love women, women love children, children love hamsters.

Alice Thomas Ellis

The only place you're sure to find love is at the end of a letter from your mother.

Bruce Lansky

Here's to the happiest hours of my life, spent in the arms of another man's wife – my mother.

Drinking toast

Thanks Mum!

Anything I am and anything I hope to be, I have my mom to thank.

Colin Farrell, actor

For me you are the most beautiful and wonderful person in the whole world: merely the fact that you are alive makes the whole world different.

Isak Dinesen, letter to her mother

Your mother created you, so you always owe her and can never repay the debt. Being born is like asking Don Corleone a favour.

Dennis Miller

Thank you, Mother – for whatever you did.

Carol Channing, acceptance speech on winning a Tony Award for Hello, Dolly, *1964*

I love my mother for all the times she said absolutely nothing… Thinking back on it all, it must have been the most difficult part of mothering she ever had to do: knowing the outcome, yet feeling she had no right to keep me from charting my own path. I thank her for all her virtues, but mostly for never once having said, 'I told you so.'

Erma Bombeck

Whatever beauty or poetry is to be found in my little book is owing to your interest in and encouragement of all my efforts from the first to the last; and if ever I do anything to be proud of, my greatest happiness will be that I can thank you for that, as I may do for all the good there is in me.

Louisa May Alcott

Just about the time a mother

thinks her job is done, she

becomes a grandmother.

Edward H. Dreschnack

Index

Index

Rosemarie Jarski has compiled many humour collections, but given the subject, this one was truly a labour of love. She tested the funniness of each quote by reading it aloud to her dad. If he laughed, she threw it out. If he looked blank – or, better yet, aghast – she included it. So, if any line failed to raise a smile, just do what we all do: blame Dad.